CASSEROLES & STEWS

Edited by Norma MacMillan and Wendy James
Home economist Gilly Cubitt

ORBIS PUBLISHING London

Introduction

A nourishing casserole is so often the perfect family supper.
Some of these recipes enable you to use the cheaper
ingredients which benefit from slow cooking, or leftovers,
while others provide the perfect dinner party dish.

Both imperial and metric measures are given for each recipe;
you should follow only one set of measures as they are not
direct conversions. All spoon measures are level unless
otherwise stated. Pastry quantities are based on the amount
of flour used. Dried herbs may be substituted for fresh
herbs: use one-third of the quantity.

Photographs were supplied by Editions Atlas, Editions Atlas/Cedus,
Editions Atlas/Masson, Editions Atlas/Zadora, Archivio IGDA, Lavinia
Press Agency, Orbis GmbH, Wales Tourist Board

The material in this book has previously appeared in *The Complete Cook*

First published 1981 in Great Britain by Orbis Publishing Limited,
20–22 Bedfordbury, London WC2

© EDIPEM, Novara 1976
© 1978, 1979, 1980, 1981 Orbis Publishing, London

ISBN 0-85613-372-8
Printed in Singapore

Contents

Basque cod casserole

Overall timing 1 hour

Freezing Not suitable

To serve 4-6

1 lb	Cod fillets	450 g
	Bouquet garni	
	Salt and pepper	
4	Large potatoes	4
2	Hard-boiled eggs	2
3	Tomatoes	3
3 oz	Butter	75 g
3	Garlic cloves	3
2 oz	Black olives	50 g
2 tbsp	Capers	2x15 ml
1 tbsp	Chopped parsley	15 ml
2 tbsp	Lemon juice	2x15 ml

Place cod in a saucepan and cover with water. Add bouquet garni and seasoning and bring slowly to the boil. Remove pan from heat and leave to cool.

Meanwhile, cook unpeeled potatoes in boiling salted water for 30 minutes. Drain well, then peel and slice potatoes. Shell and slice eggs. Blanch, peel and chop tomatoes.

Melt 1 oz (25 g) butter in a pan and fry tomatoes. Season with salt and pepper.

Preheat the oven to 400°F (200°C) Gas 6.

Arrange egg slices around side of greased soufflé dish and make layers of the potatoes, drained and chopped fish, and the peeled and crushed garlic. Spread tomatoes over top. Dot with remaining butter and bake for 20 minutes.

Garnish with black olives, capers and chopped parsley and sprinkle with lemon juice. Serve hot or cold.

Haddock creole

Overall timing 1 hour

Freezing Not suitable

To serve 4

1	Onion	1
1	Garlic clove	1
1	Red pepper	1
1	Green pepper	1
1 oz	Butter	25 g
2 tbsp	Oil	2x15 ml
14 oz	Can of tomatoes	397 g
	Salt and pepper	
2 lb	Haddock fillets	900 g
3 tbsp	Lemon juice	3x15 ml
	Chopped parsley	

Preheat the oven to 375°F (190°C) Gas 5.

Peel and chop onion and garlic. Deseed and slice peppers. Heat the butter and oil in a pan. Add onion, garlic and peppers and fry gently for 10 minutes.

Add tomatoes and mash with a wooden spoon to break them up. Season with salt and pepper. Bring to the boil and simmer gently for 10 minutes.

Place half tomato mixture in ovenproof dish, add haddock and season with salt and pepper. Sprinkle with lemon juice and cover with remaining tomato mixture.

Cover with lid or foil and bake for about 25 minutes. Sprinkle with chopped parsley and serve with plain boiled rice.

Flemish cod

Overall timing 45 minutes

Freezing Not suitable

To serve 4

4x7 oz	Cod fillets	4x200 g
3 oz	Butter	75 g
2	Lemons	2
3	Onions	3
1 tbsp	Chopped parsley	15 ml
1 tbsp	Chopped fresh dill	15 ml
	Salt and pepper	
	Fish seasoning	
$\frac{1}{4}$ pint	Dry white wine	150 ml
6 tbsp	Fresh white breadcrumbs	6x15 ml

Preheat the oven to 425°F (220°C) Gas 7.

Cut cod fillets into 2 inch (5 cm) pieces. Grease an ovenproof dish with 1 oz (25 g) of the butter. Place fish pieces in dish.

Peel and thinly slice lemons and onions and arrange on top of fish. Sprinkle fish with the herbs, salt, pepper and fish seasoning. Pour the wine over and sprinkle breadcrumbs on top. Dot with remaining butter.

Bake for 25 minutes. Serve hot with buttered boiled potatoes and a pepper and tomato salad dressed with vinaigrette.

Breton fish stew

Overall timing 1 hour

Freezing Suitable: add garlic after reheating

To serve 6

3 lb	Mixed fish	1.4 kg
2 lb	Potatoes	900 g
2	Onions	2
2 oz	Spinach	50 g
3	Leeks	3
2 oz	Butter	50 g
1 tbsp	Plain flour	15 ml
$\frac{3}{4}$ pint	White wine or cider	400 ml
	Bouquet garni	
	Salt and pepper	
2	Garlic cloves	2
2 tbsp	Chopped parsley	2x15 ml
2 tbsp	Oil	2x15 ml
2 tbsp	Lemon juice	2x15 ml
6	Slices of bread	6

Scale and clean fish. Put fish trimmings in a pan with 2 pints (1.1 litres) water and simmer for 10 minutes. Strain fish stock.

Cut fish into pieces. Peel and thickly slice potatoes. Peel and finely chop onions. Chop spinach and leeks. Melt butter in a heavy-based pan. Add onions, spinach and leeks. Cook gently for 2 minutes. Stir in flour, then add wine or cider and fish stock. Bring to the boil. Add potatoes, bouquet garni and seasoning, cover and simmer for 20 minutes.

Add fish and peeled and crushed garlic. Cook, uncovered, for 10 minutes till fish is tender.

Remove fish and potatoes from pan with a draining spoon. Sprinkle with parsley, oil and lemon juice and keep warm. Place bread in tureen and pour over soup. Serve as separate courses.

Fish paella

Overall timing 45 minutes

Freezing Not suitable

To serve 6

1	Large onion	1
2	Garlic cloves	2
4 tbsp	Oil	4x15 ml
1 lb	Long grain rice	450 g
14 oz	Can of tomatoes	397 g
4	Saffron strands	4
3½ pints	Chicken stock or water	2 litres
	Salt and pepper	
1½ lb	White fish fillets	700 g
1	Red pepper	1
14 oz	Can of artichoke hearts	397 g
14 oz	Can of broad beans	397 g
8 oz	Frozen peas	225 g

Peel and chop the onion. Peel and crush the garlic. Heat the oil in a flameproof casserole, add the onion and fry till transparent. Add the rice and garlic and fry, stirring, for 2 minutes.

Add the tomatoes and juice, the saffron, stock or water and seasoning and bring to the boil. Reduce the heat and simmer for 10 minutes.

Meanwhile, cut the fish into chunks. Halve and deseed the pepper and cut into 1 inch (2.5 cm) pieces. Drain the artichoke hearts and cut in half lengthways. Drain the beans.

Add all these ingredients to the pan with the peas and mix lightly. Cover and cook for a further 10 minutes till the rice is tender and the liquid is absorbed. Fluff the mixture with a fork. Taste and adjust seasoning. Serve immediately.

Hake in mushroom sauce

Overall timing 45 minutes

Freezing Not suitable

To serve 4

1	Garlic clove	1
4 oz	Button mushrooms	125 g
4 tbsp	Oil	4x15 ml
3 tbsp	Chopped onion	3x15 ml
¼ pint	Dry white wine or cider	150 ml
2 tbsp	Tomato purée	2x15 ml
2 tbsp	Chopped parsley	2x15 ml
	Salt and pepper	
4	Small cleaned hake	4
2 oz	Butter	50 g
2 tbsp	Fresh breadcrumbs	2x15 ml
1 tbsp	Lemon juice	15 ml

Preheat oven to 400°F (200°C) Gas 6.

Peel and crush garlic. Slice the mushrooms. Heat the oil in a saucepan. Add onion and garlic and cook for 5 minutes. Add the wine or cider and tomato purée and stir well. Add mushrooms and parsley. Cook for 5 minutes over low heat, then season with salt and pepper.

Pour half the sauce into ovenproof dish. Arrange hake on top and cover with remaining sauce. Melt the butter. Pour half over fish, sprinkle with breadcrumbs, then add the remaining butter.

Cover dish with lid or foil and bake for 20–30 minutes. Sprinkle with lemon juice and serve with extra lemon wedges and creamed potatoes.

Bobotie

Overall timing 1 hour 40 minutes

Freezing Not suitable

To serve 8

2 oz	**Fresh** breadcrumbs	50 g
$\frac{1}{4}$ pint	Milk	150 ml
2 oz	Dried apricots	50 g
3	Onions	3
2 oz	Butter	50 g
2 teasp	Curry powder	2x5 ml
12	Split almonds	12
3 tbsp	Lemon juice	3x15 ml
	Salt	
2 teasp	Granulated sugar	2x5 ml
2 oz	Seedless raisins	50 g
2 lb	Minced beef	900 g
2	Eggs	2
2	Bay leaves	2

Preheat the oven to 375°F (190°C) Gas 5.

Soak the breadcrumbs in half the milk. Chop the dried apricots. Peel and finely chop the onions. Melt the butter in a frying pan and fry the onions for 3–4 minutes. Add curry powder and almonds and fry, stirring, for 1 minute. Add lemon juice, salt, sugar, dried apricots and raisins and simmer for 3 minutes.

Put the minced beef into a large bowl. Squeeze out the breadcrumbs and add to the beef with the mixture from the frying pan. Add one of the eggs and mix well.

Press the mixture into a greased ovenproof dish. Press the bay leaves into the mixture and smooth the top. Beat the remaining egg with the remaining milk, and pour over the meat. Bake for 45 minutes.

Serve hot with boiled rice and side dishes of coconut, and mango chutney.

Beef with onions

Overall timing 1½ hours

Freezing Suitable

To serve 4

1½ lb	Chuck steak	700 g
12 oz	Onions	350 g
1 oz	Butter	25 g
1 tbsp	Oil	15 ml
1 tbsp	Plain flour	15 ml
½ pint	Beef stock	300 ml
1	Garlic clove	1
½ teasp	Ground cumin	2.5 ml
	Pinch of dried marjoram	
2 tbsp	Wine vinegar	2x15 ml
	Salt and pepper	

Cut meat across the grain into thin finger-length strips. Peel onions, slice crossways and separate rings. Heat the butter and oil in frying pan. Add the onion rings and cook, covered, over a low heat till transparent. Turn them over frequently so that they cook evenly but do not brown. Remove from pan.

Increase heat, put strips of meat into pan and brown them. Return onion rings. Sprinkle with flour and stir. When flour begins to colour, stir in stock, peeled and crushed garlic, cumin, marjoram, wine vinegar and seasoning. Cover and simmer for 1 hour. Serve with potatoes or rice and a crisp mixed salad.

Boeuf bourguignonne

Overall timing 2¾ hours plus marination

Freezing Suitable

To serve 6

3½ lb	Braising beef	1.6 kg
3 oz	Pork fat	75 g
2 tbsp	Brandy	2x15 ml
8 oz	Pickling onions	225 g
4 oz	Button mushrooms	125 g
2 oz	Butter	50 g
1 tbsp	Oil	15 ml
3 tbsp	Plain flour	3x15 ml
1	Garlic clove	1
	Bouquet garni	
	Salt and pepper	
Marinade		
1	Large onion	1
1	Carrot	1
1–2	Cloves	1–2
6	Peppercorns	6
3 tbsp	Oil	3x15 ml
25 fl oz	Bottle of red wine	700 ml

For marinade, peel and chop onion and carrot. Mix with rest of marinade ingredients. Cut beef into 2 inch (5 cm) cubes, add to bowl and marinate overnight.

Pour boiling water over pork fat. Leave for 2–3 minutes, then drain and dry. Cut into thin strips and put back into bowl. Sprinkle with brandy.

Peel pickling onions. Cook with mushrooms in butter for 10 minutes.

Drain meat cubes, reserving marinade, and pat dry. Heat oil in a flameproof casserole and brown meat on all sides. Sprinkle with flour and brown. Add peeled and crushed garlic, pork fat and brandy. Cook for 2 minutes, then ignite. Add reserved strained marinade, bouquet garni and seasoning. Cover tightly and simmer for 2 hours. Add onions and mushrooms 15 minutes before end of cooking.

Braised beef with pumpkin

Overall timing 2½ hours

Freezing Not suitable

To serve 6

2 lb	Top rump of beef	900 g
1	Onion	1
2 tbsp	Oil	2x15 ml
¼ pint	Beef stock	150 ml
	Salt and pepper	
1¼ lb	Pumpkin	600 g
3 fl oz	Dry white wine	90 ml

Preheat the oven to 325°F (170°C) Gas 3.

Tie the meat into a neat shape with fine string. Peel and thinly slice the onion. Heat the oil in a flameproof casserole, add onion and fry till transparent. Add the meat and fry over a high heat till browned all over.

Add the stock and seasoning, cover and cook in the oven for 1 hour.

Meanwhile, to prepare the pumpkin, scrape out the seeds and fibrous centre. Remove the skin and cut the flesh into chunks. Add to the casserole with the wine. Cover and cook for a further 1 hour till the meat is tender. Taste and adjust seasoning.

Remove the string, slice the meat thickly and arrange in a warmed serving dish. Arrange the pumpkin around meat and spoon juices over. Serve immediately with creamed potatoes and a green vegetable.

Chilli con carne

Overall timing 3¼ hours plus overnight soaking

Freezing Suitable

To serve 4–6

8 oz	Dried brown or red beans	225 g
1¾ pints	Water	1 litre
2 lb	Braising steak	900 g
1	Onion	1
1 tbsp	Pork dripping or olive oil	15 ml
1 oz	Butter	25 g
	Salt and pepper	
1 teasp	Chilli powder	5 ml
1 tbsp	Sweet paprika	15 ml
8 oz	Canned tomatoes	225 g
2 teasp	Cornflour (optional)	2x5 ml

Soak beans in water overnight. The next day, place water and beans in saucepan, cover and cook gently for 1½ hours.

Cut the beef into 1 inch (2.5 cm) cubes. Peel and chop onion. Heat the dripping or oil and butter in frying pan. Add the beef. Cook till brown, then add the onion and cook till transparent.

Mix the meat and onion in with the cooked beans and season with salt, pepper, chilli powder and paprika. Cover and cook gently for 1 hour.

Add the drained tomatoes, cover and cook for 30 minutes more. Adjust seasoning. If you wish to thicken the sauce, blend the cornflour with a little water and add it to the mixture. Cook for a few minutes, then serve from the cooking pot with plain boiled rice or chunks of wholemeal bread and a crisp green salad.

Goulash

Overall timing 2¼ hours

Freezing Suitable

To serve 6

2 lb	Stewing beef	900 g
2 oz	Pork dripping	50 g
8 oz	Onions	225 g
2	Garlic cloves	2
1 tbsp	Plain flour	15 ml
1	Beef stock cube	1
1 pint	Boiling water	560 ml
	Salt and pepper	
½ teasp	Dried marjoram	2.5 ml
½ teasp	Caraway seed	2.5 ml
	Brown sugar	
½ teasp	Paprika	2.5 ml
8 oz	Potatoes	225 g
2	Green peppers	2
5	Tomatoes	5
¼ pint	Red wine	150 ml
¼ pint	Carton of soured cream (optional)	150 ml

Cube beef. Heat dripping in a large saucepan. Add beef and fry till meat is brown on all sides. Peel and chop onions and garlic. Add to meat and cook till transparent.

Sprinkle in flour and stir into mixture. Mix stock cube into boiling water and pour over meat. Season with salt, pepper, marjoram, caraway seed, a pinch of sugar and paprika. Cover tightly and cook gently for 1¼ hours.

Peel and roughly chop the potatoes. Deseed and slice peppers. Blanch, peel and chop tomatoes. Add all to pan, cover and cook for a further 25 minutes.

Add wine and check seasoning. Bring to simmering point and stir in soured cream, if using, or serve it separately.

Beef with sweetcorn and beans

Overall timing 1 hour

Freezing Not suitable

To serve 4

1 lb	Blade bone steak	450 g
2	Onions	2
3 tbsp	Oil	3x15 ml
	Salt and pepper	
	Paprika	
1½ pints	Stock	850 ml
3 oz	Long grain rice	75 g
11 oz	Green beans	300 g
8 oz	Button mushrooms	225 g
1 lb	Canned or frozen sweetcorn kernels	450 g
4	Tomatoes	4

Cut meat into strips across the grain with a sharp knife. Peel and finely chop the onions. Heat oil in flameproof casserole. Brown meat for 5 minutes, then add the onions. Cook onions till golden, then season with salt, pepper and paprika. Add the stock and rice and stir well.

Top and tail green beans and cut into short lengths. Add to casserole and cook for 15 minutes.

Add mushrooms and drained sweetcorn to casserole with blanched, peeled and quartered tomatoes. Cook for a further 15 minutes. Serve in warmed bowls.

Braised beef with vegetables

Overall timing 2¾ hours

Freezing Not suitable

To serve 6–8

8 oz	Carrots	225 g
2	Onions	2
2	Stalks of celery	2
	Salt and pepper	
3 tbsp	Plain flour	3 x 15 ml
2½ lb	"Leg of mutton" cut of beef	1.1 kg
4 oz	Butter	125 g
¼ teasp	Dried thyme	1.25 ml
1	Bay leaf	1
1 tbsp	Tomato purée	15 ml
¼ pint	Red wine	150 ml
¼ pint	Beef stock	150 ml
1½ lb	Potatoes	700 g

Preheat the oven to 325°F (170°C) Gas 3.

Peel and dice carrots and onions; dice celery. Season flour and coat meat. Melt butter in flameproof casserole and brown meat quickly on all sides. Remove from pan.

Add prepared vegetables to casserole and stir till coated with butter. Cover and cook for 5 minutes, shaking pan frequently to prevent sticking. Stir in the herbs, tomato purée, red wine and stock. Return meat to casserole. Season, cover and cook in the oven for 2 hours till meat is tender.

Meanwhile, peel and chop potatoes. Cook in boiling, salted water till tender. Drain and keep hot.

Remove meat from casserole and keep hot. Pour cooking liquor through a sieve into a saucepan. Reserve half the vegetables and rub rest through sieve into liquor. Stir in reserved vegetables and reheat.

Cut meat into thick slices and arrange on a warmed serving dish with potatoes. Spoon over sauce and serve.

Beef and split pea stew

Overall timing 2 hours plus soaking

Freezing Not suitable

To serve 6

12 oz	Split peas	350 g
1	Onion	1
1½ lb	Braising steak	700 g
1 oz	Butter	25 g
2 tbsp	Oil	2x15 ml
2	Large carrots	2
	Bouquet garni	
¼ teasp	Grated nutmeg	1.25 ml
1½ pints	Beef stock	850 ml
	Salt and pepper	
8 oz	Potatoes	225 g
8 oz	Fresh spinach	225 g

Wash and pick over the split peas and put into a saucepan of cold water. Bring to the boil and boil for 2 minutes. Remove from the heat, cover and leave to soak for 2 hours.

Peel and chop the onion. Cut the meat into bite-size pieces. Heat the butter and oil in a flameproof casserole and fry the onion and meat till lightly browned.

Drain the split peas and add to the meat. Scrape the carrots, slice thinly and add to the pan with the bouquet garni, grated nutmeg and stock. Add seasoning and bring to the boil. Reduce the heat, cover and simmer for 1 hour.

Peel and dice the potatoes. Chop the spinach and add both to the meat. Cook for a further 30 minutes. Taste and adjust the seasoning. Serve with creamed potatoes and a green vegetable or boiled rice, or with crusty bread for a lighter meal.

Sautéed veal with olives

Overall timing 1¾ hours

Freezing Not suitable

To serve 4

1 lb	Pie veal	450 g
12 oz	Tomatoes	350 g
8 oz	Garlic sausage	225 g
1	Onion	1
1	Garlic clove	1
3 tbsp	Oil	3x15 ml
¼ pint	Dry white wine	150 ml
½ pint	Light stock	300 ml
	Salt and pepper	
8 oz	Button onions	225 g
2 oz	Stoned green olives	50 g

Wipe and trim the veal and cut into 1 inch (2.5 cm) pieces. Blanch, peel and chop the tomatoes. Thinly slice the sausage. Peel and chop the onion. Peel and crush the garlic.

Heat 2 tbsp (2x15 ml) of the oil in a flame-proof casserole and fry the garlic and onion till transparent. Add the veal and fry till brown on all sides. Add the wine, increase the heat and reduce the liquid by half. Stir in the tomatoes and stock. Season, cover and simmer for 1 hour.

Peel the button onions. Heat the remaining oil in a frying pan and fry onions, stirring, till golden. Stir into the casserole with the sausage and olives. Cover and cook for a further 15 minutes till the onions are tender.

Taste and adjust the seasoning and serve immediately with rice or jacket potatoes and a green salad.

Leftover beef stew

Overall timing 50 minutes

Freezing Not suitable

To serve 4

2	Large onions	2
2 oz	Dripping or butter	50 g
1 lb	Cold roast beef	450 g
12 oz	Carrots	350 g
½ pint	Strong beef stock	300 ml
	Salt and pepper	
1 teasp	Cornflour	5 ml
1 tbsp	Vinegar	15 ml
1 tbsp	Water	15 ml
1 tbsp	Chopped parsley	15 ml

Peel and thinly slice onions. Melt fat in a saucepan and fry onions till golden brown.

Meanwhile, trim any fat from beef and cut into small cubes. Peel and slice carrots. Add both to pan and fry, stirring, for 5 minutes. Add stock and seasoning and bring to the boil. Cover and simmer for 20 minutes.

Blend cornflour with vinegar and water and stir into stew. Simmer till thickened. Adjust seasoning to taste, place on a warmed serving dish and sprinkle with parsley.

Swiss beef casserole

Overall timing 2¼ hours

Freezing Suitable: omit potatoes

To serve 4

2 lb	Blade bone steak	900 g
4 tbsp	Oil	4x15 ml
3 tbsp	Plain flour	3x15 ml
1 tbsp	Paprika	15 ml
4	Large onions	4
2	Garlic cloves	2
2 tbsp	Tomato purée	2x15 ml
¼ pint	Red wine	150 ml
12 fl oz	Hot beef stock	350 ml
	Salt and pepper	
	Pinch of sugar	
3	Bay leaves	3
4	Cloves	4
1 lb	Small potatoes	450 g
12 oz	Young carrots	350 g

Cut meat into cubes. Heat oil in saucepan. Add meat, brown on all sides, then sprinkle with flour and paprika.

Peel and chop onions; peel and crush garlic. Add to pan with tomato purée and wine. Cook for 5 minutes, then add stock, seasoning, sugar, bay leaves and cloves. Cover and cook for 1 hour.

Peel and quarter potatoes; peel carrots. Add to pan and cook for a further 30 minutes.

Veal in cream sauce

Overall timing 1¾ hours

Freezing Not suitable

To serve 6

2 lb	Lean veal	900 g
1	Veal knuckle	1
1	Large onion	1
1	Large carrot	1
	Bouquet garni	
12 oz	Button onions	350 g
3 oz	Butter	75 g
8 oz	Button mushrooms	225 g
3 tbsp	Plain flour	3x15 ml
1 tbsp	Lemon juice	15 ml
	Salt and pepper	
3	Egg yolks	3
¼ pint	Single cream	150 ml

Cut veal into 2 inch (5 cm) pieces. Crack knuckle and put into pan with meat. Add peeled onion, carrot, bouquet garni and 2½ pints (1.5 litres) water. Simmer for 1 hour.

Blanch button onions in boiling water for 10 minutes. Peel and cook in 1 oz (25 g) butter and ¼ pint (150 ml) of liquid from veal. Add mushrooms and cook for 5 minutes.

Remove veal; strain cooking liquor. Remove meat from knuckle and return to pan with veal, onions and mushrooms.

Melt remaining butter, add flour and 1½ pints (850 ml) of reserved liquor and simmer till thickened. Add lemon juice and seasoning. Add to veal and cook for 5 minutes. Beat yolks with cream and stir into veal.

Spring veal casserole

Overall timing 2 hours

Freezing Not suitable

To serve 6

2 lb	Lean veal	900 g
	Salt and pepper	
4 tbsp	Plain flour	4x15 ml
4 tbsp	Oil	4x15 ml
½ pint	Chicken stock	300 ml
4	Spring onions	4
2 lb	Fresh peas	900 g
1	Small round lettuce	1
8 oz	Fresh or canned asparagus	225 g
2 oz	Butter	50 g
1 tbsp	Chopped parsley	15 ml

Cut veal into large cubes. Toss in seasoned flour. Heat oil in saucepan and brown all over. Pour off any excess oil, then add stock and seasoning. Cover and simmer for 1 hour.

Meanwhile, cut onions into 1 inch (2.5 cm) lengths. Shell peas. Shred lettuce. Chop asparagus. Melt butter in pan, add vegetables, cover and cook for 5 minutes. Stir into veal; simmer for 30 minutes. Add parsley and serve.

Osso bucco

Overall timing 2¼ hours

Freezing Not suitable

To serve 4

	Salt and pepper	
3 tbsp	Plain flour	3x15 ml
4	Thick slices of shin of veal	4
2 oz	Butter	50 g
2 tbsp	Oil	2x15 ml
¼ pint	Dry white wine	150 ml
1 lb	Tomatoes	450 g
¼ pint	Stock	150 ml
	Sprigs of parsley and thyme	
1	Bay leaf	1
2	Lemons	2
1–2	Garlic cloves	1–2
	Sprigs of rosemary	

Preheat the oven to 350°F (180°C) Gas 4.

Season the flour and use to coat meat well on all sides. Heat the butter and oil in a flameproof casserole. Add the veal and fry till browned on both sides. Add the wine and cook for 10 minutes.

Blanch, peel and chop tomatoes and add to casserole. Cook for 5 minutes. Add stock and parsley, thyme and bay leaf tied together. Cover and cook in the oven for 2 hours till meat is very tender.

Meanwhile, thinly pare the rind from the lemons. Peel the garlic. Finely chop the lemon rind and garlic with a few sprigs of rosemary and parsley.

Remove casserole from oven and discard herb bouquet. Skim off any excess fat. Taste and adjust seasoning. Lift the veal out and arrange on a warmed serving dish. Pour cooking liquor over and sprinkle lemon rind mixture on top.

Sweet and sour veal

Overall timing 2 hours

Freezing Suitable

To serve 4

2 lb	Pie veal	900 g
1	Carrot	1
1	Stalk of celery	1
1 tbsp	Chopped parsley	15 ml
2	Bay leaves	2
	Salt and pepper	
Sauce		
2 oz	Butter	50 g
2 tbsp	Plain flour	2x15 ml
1	Thin-skinned lemon	1
2 oz	Sultanas	50 g
1 teasp	Sugar	5 ml
2 tbsp	Dry white wine	2x15 ml

Cut meat into neat pieces if necessary. Scrape carrot and cut in half. Trim and chop celery. Place meat in a large saucepan with prepared vegetables, parsley, bay leaves and seasoning. Just cover with water and simmer, covered, for 1½ hours or till meat is tender.

To make the sauce, melt butter in a saucepan. Stir in flour and cook for 3–4 minutes until lightly browned. Gradually add 1 pint (560 ml) of the meat cooking liquor and bring to the boil, stirring.

Wipe and thinly slice the lemon, discarding any pips. Add to sauce with sultanas, sugar and wine. Mix well.

Drain the meat, discarding vegetables, and add to the sauce. Simmer for 15 minutes, stirring occasionally. Taste and adjust seasoning. Serve hot with potatoes or rice.

Czech veal with caraway seeds

Overall timing 1 hour

Freezing Suitable: thicken with cornflour after reheating

To serve 4

1¾ lb	Pie veal	750 g
4 tbsp	Oil	4x15 ml
1 tbsp	White wine or cider vinegar	15 ml
½ teasp	Salt	2.5 ml
2 teasp	Paprika	2x5 ml
9 fl oz	Buttermilk	250 ml
1 tbsp	Caraway seeds	15 ml
1	Large cooking apple	1
2 teasp	Sugar	2x5 ml
1 tbsp	Cornflour	15 ml
2 tbsp	Water	2x15 ml

Cut the meat into 1 inch (2.5 cm) cubes. Heat the oil in a large heavy-based pan and fry one third of the meat at a time, removing it with a draining spoon when lightly browned.

Return all the meat to the pan. Mix the vinegar, salt and paprika together and gradually stir in the buttermilk. Pour the mixture over the meat. Add the lightly crushed caraway seeds. Cover and cook for 20 minutes.

Peel, core and thickly slice the apple and add to the veal with the sugar. Cook uncovered for 20 minutes.

Blend the cornflour and cold water until smooth and add to the meat. Stir well and cook gently for 2 minutes. Serve with boiled rice or new potatoes and courgettes or salad.

Belgian veal and kidney pie

Overall timing 2½ hours

Freezing Not suitable

To serve 4–6

3 tbsp	Oil	3x15 ml
1 lb	Pie veal	450 g
1	Garlic clove	1
1	Bay leaf	1
1	Clove	1
	Salt and pepper	
8 oz	Calves' kidneys	225 g
1 lb	Potatoes	450 g
1 lb	Onions	450 g
½ pint	Beef stock	300 ml
½ pint	Light ale or lager	300 ml

Preheat the oven to 325°F (170°C) Gas 3.

Heat oil in frying pan and fry veal with peeled and crushed garlic for 5 minutes. Turn mixture into casserole and add bay leaf, clove and seasoning.

Prepare and slice kidneys thinly. Arrange in layer on top of veal. Season. Peel and slice potatoes. Arrange over kidneys and season. Peel and slice onions in rings and place on top. Pour stock and beer over.

Cover and bake for 1½ hours. Remove lid and bake for 30 minutes more. Serve hot with baby carrots and peas.

Veal Marengo

Overall timing 2 hours

Freezing Suitable

To serve 4

1 oz	Butter	25 g
1 tbsp	Oil	15 ml
1 lb	Pie veal	450 g
1	Small onion	1
1	Carrot	1
1 oz	Plain flour	25 g
4	Ripe tomatoes	4
4 oz	Button onions	125 g
1 teasp	Tomato purée	5 ml
4 fl oz	Dry white wine	120 ml
4 fl oz	Water	120 ml
2	Garlic cloves	2
	Bouquet garni	
	Salt and pepper	
4 oz	Mushrooms	125 g

Heat the butter and oil in flameproof casserole. Add the veal and brown on all sides over a high heat. Peel and chop onion. Peel and slice carrot. Add both to pan. Sprinkle with flour and stir until flour turns golden.

Blanch, peel and chop the tomatoes. Peel button onions. Add to the pan with tomato purée, wine, water, peeled and crushed garlic, bouquet garni and seasoning. Cover and simmer for 1½ hours.

Slice mushrooms and add to pan. Cover and cook for a further 15 minutes, stirring occasionally.

Remove bouquet garni. Serve with buttered noodles, mashed potatoes or plain, boiled rice.

Variation

This may also be made with chicken – use 1½ lb (700 g) chicken pieces.

Veal with sage

Overall timing 1¾ hours

Freezing Not suitable

To serve 4

1½ lb	Boned shoulder of veal	700 g
1	Large onion	1
2 tbsp	Oil	2x15 ml
2 oz	Butter	50 g
1	Garlic clove	1
2	Sprigs of fresh sage	2
	Salt and pepper	
8 oz	Can of tomatoes	227 g
¾ pint	Light stock	400 ml
1¼ lb	Waxy potatoes	600 g

Cut veal into 1½ inch (4 cm) cubes. Peel and chop the onion. Heat the oil and butter in a flameproof casserole, add the veal and fry till browned. Peel and crush the garlic and add to the pan with the onion, sage and seasoning. Fry, stirring, for 3 minutes.

Rub the tomatoes and juice through a sieve into the pan, add the stock and bring to the boil, stirring. Cover and simmer for 1 hour, stirring occasionally.

Peel the potatoes and cut into quarters. Stir into the stew, cover and simmer for about 20 minutes till tender.

Discard the sage; taste and adjust the seasoning. Garnish with fresh sage and serve with green vegetables.

Braised lamb with green beans

Overall timing 1¾ hours

Freezing Suitable: cook for only 1 hour; reheat from frozen in 400°F (200°C) Gas 6 oven for 1½ hours

To serve 4

1½ lb	Green beans	700 g
2 tbsp	Oil	2x15 ml
2 lb	Scrag end of lamb chops	900 g
2	Large onions	2
14 oz	Can of tomatoes	397 g
	Salt and pepper	
¼ teasp	Ground allspice	1.25 ml
¼ teasp	Grated nutmeg	1.25 ml
2	Red peppers	2

Preheat oven to 350°F (180°C) Gas 4.

Wash, top and tail beans and, if necessary, remove strings. Cut into 2 inch (5 cm) lengths. Spread over the bottom of large ovenproof dish.

Heat oil in a large frying pan. Trim lamb, removing excess fat. Fry in oil until brown on all sides. Drain and arrange on top of beans in casserole.

Peel onions and cut into wedges. Fry in oil until golden. With a spoon, break up the tomatoes in their juice. Add to onions with salt, pepper, allspice and nutmeg, stir well and cook for 5 minutes.

Deseed and slice peppers and add to casserole with tomato mixture. Cover tightly and cook in oven for 1½ hours. Serve with boiled rice.

French lamb hot-pot

Overall timing 1¾ hours

Freezing Not suitable

To serve 4

4 oz	Streaky bacon	125 g
2	Onions	2
1 oz	Butter	25 g
2 tbsp	Oil	2x15 ml
2½ lb	Neck of lamb chops	1.1 kg
1 tbsp	Plain flour	15 ml
¾ pint	Light stock	400 ml
1 lb	Turnips	450 g
1 lb	Potatoes	450 g
2	Garlic cloves	2
1 teasp	Caster sugar	5 ml
	Bouquet garni	
	Salt and pepper	
4	Large tomatoes	4

Derind the bacon and cut into strips. Peel onions and slice into thin rings. Heat the butter and oil in a saucepan and fry the bacon and onions. Add lamb and fry over a high heat till browned on both sides. Sprinkle in the flour and cook, stirring, till it browns. Gradually add the stock and bring to the boil.

Peel the turnips and potatoes and cut into quarters. Add to the pan with the peeled and crushed garlic, sugar, bouquet garni and seasoning. Cover and simmer for 1¼ hours.

Remove bouquet garni. Add the tomatoes and cook for a further 15 minutes. Taste and adjust the seasoning. Arrange the meat and vegetables on a warmed serving dish and spoon the cooking liquor over. Serve immediately.

Dolma kara

Overall timing 1¾ hours

Freezing Not suitable

To serve 6

2 tbsp	Oil	2x15 ml
2	Onions	2
1 lb	Boned lamb	450 g
4 oz	Canned chickpeas	125 g
½ pint	Stock	300 ml
	Salt and pepper	
2 tbsp	Tomato purée	2x15 ml
8 oz	Minced cooked lamb	225 g
2 oz	Cooked rice	50 g
1	Egg	1
1 teasp	Lemon juice	5 ml
2 tbsp	Chopped parsley	2x15 ml
	Ground cinnamon	
1 lb	Courgettes	450 g

Heat oil in a saucepan. Peel and chop one of the onions and fry till tender. Cut the lamb into small pieces and add to the pan. Cook for 5–10 minutes.

Add the drained chickpeas, stock, salt, pepper and tomato purée. Cover and simmer for 30 minutes.

Preheat the oven to 375°F (190°C) Gas 5.

Mix the cooked lamb with the cooked rice, remaining onion, peeled and finely chopped, egg, lemon juice, half the parsley, seasoning and a pinch of cinnamon.

Trim courgettes, then cut them in half lengthways. Scoop out the seeds with a teaspoon. Blanch courgettes in boiling salted water for 5 minutes. Drain, then stuff the courgettes with the rice and lamb mixture.

Put the lamb and chickpea stew in an oven-proof dish and place stuffed courgettes on top. Cover with foil and bake for 40 minutes. Serve hot sprinkled with remaining parsley.

Lamb fricassee

Overall timing 1¼ hours

Freezing Not suitable

To serve 4

1½ lb	Boned shoulder of lamb	700 g
1	Onion	1
1	Stalk of celery	1
2 oz	Butter	50 g
1 tbsp	Plain flour	15 ml
¼ pint	Milk	150 ml
¼ pint	Stock	150 ml
1	Carrot	1
2	Sprigs of parsley	2
2	Sprigs of basil	2
2	Sprigs of sage	2
	Salt and pepper	
2	Egg yolks	2
1 tbsp	Lemon juice	15 ml

Cut the lamb into neat pieces. Peel and chop the onion. Trim and chop the celery. Melt half the butter in a flameproof casserole. Add onion and celery and fry over low heat for 5 minutes without browning.

Stir in the flour and fry until golden. Gradually add milk and stock, stirring constantly. Bring to the boil, then remove from heat.

Scrape and chop carrot. Tie in a piece of muslin with parsley, basil and sage. Add to casserole with remaining butter, the lamb and seasoning. Stir well. Cover and cook gently for 1 hour, stirring occasionally. Remove muslin bag.

Beat the egg yolks in a bowl and blend with the lemon juice. Stir gently into the fricassee until blended; do not boil. Taste and adjust seasoning, then serve with creamed potatoes and minted peas.

Greek lamb stew with spinach

Overall timing 1½ hours

Freezing Not suitable

To serve 6

2 lb	Middle neck of lamb	900 g
1	Large onion	1
2 tbsp	Oil	2 x 15 ml
1 oz	Butter	25 g
1 lb	Ripe tomatoes	450 g
2 tbsp	Tomato purée	2 x 15 ml
	Dried oregano	
	Salt and pepper	
1 pint	Hot water or stock	560 ml
1¼ lb	Spinach	600 g

Cut the lamb into bite-size pieces. Peel and thinly slice the onion. Heat the oil and butter in a flameproof casserole, add the lamb and onion and fry over a moderate heat for about 10 minutes till browned, stirring occasionally.

Blanch, peel and chop the tomatoes. Add to the pan with the tomato purée, a pinch of oregano, seasoning and water or stock. Mix well and bring to the boil. Cover and simmer for 1½ hours till the lamb is tender.

Wash spinach and shred finely. Add to the pan, stir, cover and cook for a further 10 minutes. Taste and adjust the seasoning. Pour into a warmed serving dish and serve.

Beanpot with lamb

Overall timing 2 hours 50 minutes plus overnight soaking

Freezing Not suitable

To serve 4

8 oz	Dried haricot beans	225 g
½ teasp	Salt	2.5 ml
1 oz	Dripping	25 g
1 lb	Chump lamb chops	450 g
1	Onion	1
4 tbsp	Tomato purée	4x15 ml
½ teasp	Ground cumin	2.5 ml
1	Bay leaf	1
½ teasp	Dried rosemary	2.5 ml
½ teasp	Garlic salt	2.5 ml
	Brown sugar	
½ teasp	Vinegar	2.5 ml
1 tbsp	Chopped chives	15 ml

Soak beans in 2½ pints (1.5 litres) water overnight. Next day, transfer beans and water to a saucepan, add salt and cook for 1 hour.

Melt dripping in a flameproof casserole and brown chops well on all sides. Peel and chop onion and add to casserole. Cook till transparent. Add beans and water, tomato purée, cumin, bay leaf, rosemary and garlic salt. Cover and cook for 1 hour.

Uncover and cook for a further 20 minutes till meat is tender.

Just before serving, stir in a pinch of sugar and the vinegar and sprinkle with chopped chives.

Lamb with broad beans and potatoes

Overall timing 1½ hours

Freezing Not suitable

To serve 6

4	Tomatoes	4
4 oz	Streaky bacon rashers	125 g
2	Onions	2
2	Garlic cloves	2
2 tbsp	Oil	2x15 ml
6	Lamb blade chops	6
½ pint	Stock	300 ml
1 tbsp	Lemon juice	15 ml
½ teasp	Dried thyme	2.5 ml
	Salt and pepper	
1½ lb	Shelled broad beans	700 g
1½ lb	Potatoes	700 g

Blanch, peel and chop tomatoes. Derind and chop bacon. Peel and slice onions. Peel and crush garlic. Heat oil in a flameproof casserole and fry onion and garlic till transparent. Add the chops and bacon and brown on all sides.

Add tomatoes, stock, lemon juice, thyme and seasoning. Cover and simmer for 30 minutes.

Blanch beans in boiling water for 5 minutes, then drain. Peel and slice the potatoes. Add potatoes to casserole and cook for 10 minutes. Add beans and cook for a further 15 minutes. Serve immediately.

Chilli lamb bake

Overall timing 1½ hours

Freezing Not suitable

To serve 6

1	Aubergine	1
	Salt and pepper	
1 tbsp	Oil	15 ml
2 lb	Lean minced lamb	900 g
1 tbsp	Plain flour	15 ml
¼ pint	Chicken stock	150 ml
¼ pint	Red wine	150 ml
1	Garlic clove	1
½ teasp	Tabasco	2.5 ml
3	Large onions	3
2 oz	Butter	50 g
1 tbsp	Chopped parsley	15 ml
4 oz	Cottage cheese	125 g
2 tbsp	Grated Parmesan cheese	2x15 ml
4 tbsp	Dried breadcrumbs	4x15 ml

Cut aubergine into small chunks. Sprinkle with salt and leave to drain for 10 minutes.

Heat the oil in a saucepan, add the lamb and fry till browned all over.

Rinse the aubergine under cold water and drain thoroughly, squeezing to remove all moisture. Add to the lamb and fry for 5 minutes. Stir in the flour and cook for 1 minute. Gradually add the stock and wine and bring to the boil. Stir in the peeled and crushed garlic and Tabasco. Season and simmer for 20 minutes.

Preheat the oven to 400°F (200°C) Gas 6.

Peel and thinly slice the onions. Melt the butter in a frying pan, add the onions and fry till transparent.

Stir the parsley into the lamb mixture and pour into an ovenproof dish. Lift the onions out of the butter with a draining spoon and spread over the lamb. Mix the cheeses and breadcrumbs together, season and add a few drops of Tabasco. Spread over the onions and pour any butter left in the frying pan over. Bake for 30 minutes till the topping is crisp and golden. Serve immediately.

Spaghetti with lamb sauce

Overall timing 1¾ hours

Freezing Not suitable

To serve 4

1½ lb	Boned shoulder of lamb	700 g
	Salt and pepper	
3 tbsp	Plain flour	3x15 ml
1	Large onion	1
3 tbsp	Olive oil	3x15 ml
2 teasp	Paprika	2x5 ml
¾ pint	Chicken stock	400 ml
2 tbsp	Tomato purée	2x15 ml
12 oz	Spaghetti	350 g

Cut the lamb into bite-size pieces. Season the flour and toss the meat in it till evenly coated. Peel and thinly slice the onion. Heat the oil in a saucepan, add the onion and fry till transparent. Add the meat and fry till browned all over. Sprinkle in any remaining flour and the paprika and cook for 1 minute, stirring.

Gradually add the stock and bring to the boil, stirring constantly. Add the tomato purée and seasoning, cover and simmer gently for about 1 hour till tender.

Break the spaghetti into 4 inch (10 cm) lengths. Add 1 pint (560 ml) water to the lamb and bring to the boil. Add the spaghetti and simmer till tender, stirring frequently.

Taste and adjust seasoning. Divide between warmed individual serving dishes, arranging the meat on top. Serve immediately.

West Indian carbonnade

Overall timing 2 hours

Freezing Not suitable

To serve 6–8

3	Large onions	3
2 tbsp	Oil	2x15 ml
2 oz	Butter	50 g
3 lb	Boned shoulder of lamb	1.4 kg
3 fl oz	Dry white wine	90 ml
3 tbsp	Tomato purée	3x15 ml
	Bouquet garni	
$\frac{3}{4}$ pint	Stock	400 ml
	Salt and pepper	
2	Potatoes	2
2	Sweet potatoes	2
1	Stalk of celery	1
2	Courgettes	2
2	Apples	2
2	Pears	2

Peel and slice onions. Heat oil and butter in flameproof casserole, add onions and cook till transparent. Cut meat into chunks, add to the onions and cook over high heat till browned on all sides. Add the wine, tomato purée, bouquet garni, stock and seasoning. Stir well, cover and cook gently for about 50 minutes.

Peel potatoes and sweet potatoes and cut into chunks. Chop celery and courgettes. Add vegetables to casserole, cover and continue cooking for 30 minutes.

Peel and core apples and pears and cut into small pieces. Add to casserole and cook for a further 10 minutes. Remove bouquet garni. Serve hot with crusty bread or rice.

Summer casserole of lamb

Overall timing 1 hour

Freezing Suitable: add potatoes, beans and peas after reheating

To serve 6

8 oz	Button onions	225 g
1 oz	Butter	25 g
1 tbsp	Oil	15 ml
2½ lb	Middle neck lamb chops	1.1 kg
6	New carrots	6
2	Garlic cloves	2
1 tbsp	Plain flour	15 ml
4	Tomatoes	4
2 tbsp	Tomato purée	2x15 ml
¾ pint	Stock	400 ml
	Bouquet garni	
	Salt and pepper	
1 lb	New potatoes	450 g
2 oz	Green beans	50 g
2 oz	Peas	50 g

Peel button onions. Heat butter and oil in flameproof casserole and fry onions for 5 minutes. Remove from pan and reserve. Add chops and brown on all sides over a high heat.

Scrape carrots and halve if liked. Add to pan with peeled and crushed garlic and cook for 5 minutes. Sprinkle flour over and cook, stirring, for 3 minutes.

Blanch, peel and chop tomatoes. Add to the pan with tomato purée, stock, bouquet garni and seasoning. Cover and simmer for 30 minutes.

Scrape potatoes and add to the casserole. Cook for a further 10 minutes. Top and tail beans and cut into short lengths. Add to pan with peas and reserved onions. Cover and cook for a further 10 minutes. Taste and adjust seasoning if necessary. Discard bouquet garni and serve.

Turkish lamb stew

Overall timing 2¾ hours plus overnight soaking

Freezing Not suitable

To serve 6

12 oz	Dried chickpeas	350 g
	Bouquet garni	
2 lb	Boned shoulder of lamb	900 g
1	Onion	1
1	Garlic clove	1
2 oz	Butter	50 g
3 tbsp	Oil	3x15 ml
1 teasp	Ground cumin	5 ml
1 teasp	Ground cinnamon	5 ml
	Sprig of rosemary	
1	Bay leaf	1
	Salt and pepper	
14 oz	Can of tomatoes	397 g
2 tbsp	Lemon juice	2x15 ml
1 tbsp	Chopped parsley	15 ml

Soak chickpeas in water to cover overnight. The next day, drain chickpeas and put into saucepan. Cover with boiling water and add bouquet garni. Cover and simmer for 1 hour.

Cut the lamb into large pieces. Peel and chop the onion. Peel and crush garlic. Heat the butter and oil in flameproof casserole and fry the onion, garlic, cumin and cinnamon for 5 minutes. Add meat pieces to pan and brown on all sides.

Drain chickpeas and add to casserole with the rosemary, bay leaf, seasoning and tomatoes. Cover and cook gently for 1½ hours. Adjust seasoning and sprinkle with lemon juice and parsley just before serving.

Moussaka

Overall timing 2¼ hours

Freezing Suitable: bake from frozen in 375°F (190°C) Gas 5 oven for 1½ hours; add cheese sauce and bake 30 minutes more

To serve 6

1 lb	Onions	450 g
4	Garlic cloves	4
¼ pint	Oil	150 ml
1 tbsp	Chopped parsley	15 ml
2 lb	Minced lamb	900 g
4	Tomatoes	4
2 tbsp	Tomato purée	2x15 ml
	Salt and pepper	
¼ pint	Stock	150 ml
2 oz	Fresh breadcrumbs	50 g
2 lb	Aubergines	900 g
1 oz	Plain flour	25 g
2	Egg yolks	2
¾ pint	Thick white sauce	400 ml
4 oz	Strong cheese	125 g

Peel and chop onions; peel and crush garlic. Heat 1 tbsp (15 ml) oil in saucepan and fry onions, parsley, garlic and lamb till browned. Peel and quarter tomatoes and add to pan with tomato purée, seasoning and stock. Cover and simmer for 45 minutes. Remove from heat and stir in breadcrumbs.

Preheat oven to 350°F (180°C) Gas 4.

Thinly slice aubergines. Dust lightly with flour. Heat remaining oil in frying pan and brown aubergines. Drain on kitchen paper.

Arrange two-thirds of aubergines to cover bottom and sides of greased casserole. Add meat mixture, then top with remaining aubergines. Stir beaten egg yolks into sauce with half cheese, grated. Pour sauce over aubergines. Cover with rest of grated cheese. Put casserole in a roasting tin containing a little water. Bake for 1 hour.

Navarin

Overall timing 1¾ hours

Freezing Not suitable

To serve 6

2 oz	Butter	50 g
2½ lb	Middle neck of lamb	1.1 kg
4	Small onions	4
1 tbsp	Plain flour	15 ml
¾ pint	Stock	400 ml
3 tbsp	Tomato purée	3 x 15 ml
	Bouquet garni	
	Salt and pepper	
1 lb	Carrots	450 g
1 lb	Turnips	450 g
1 lb	Potatoes	450 g
8 oz	Frozen peas	225 g
1 tbsp	Chopped parsley	15 ml

Melt butter in flameproof casserole, add lamb and brown on all sides. Peel and quarter the onions. Add to casserole and fry gently for 5 minutes.

Sprinkle flour over and cook, stirring, for 2 minutes. Gradually stir in the stock, then add tomato purée, bouquet garni and seasoning and bring to the boil. Cover and simmer gently for 45 minutes.

Scrape and chop carrots. Peel turnips and cut into cubes. Add to casserole and cook for 15 minutes.

Meanwhile, peel potatoes and cut into chunks. Add to casserole and cook, covered, for 20 minutes. Add peas and cook for a further 10 minutes. Remove bouquet garni and adjust seasoning. Garnish with parsley and serve hot.

Braised pork with prunes

Overall timing 2 hours

Freezing Not suitable

To serve 6

2½ lb	Fillet end of leg of pork	1.1 kg
	Salt and pepper	
2 tbsp	Plain flour	2x15 ml
2	Medium-size onions	2
8 oz	Carrots	225 g
2 oz	Butter	50 g
¼ pint	Red wine	150 ml
½ pint	Beef stock	300 ml
6 oz	Small prunes	175 g
	Bouquet garni	
2 oz	Sultanas	50 g

Coat pork lightly with seasoned flour. Peel and thinly slice the onions into rings. Peel and slice the carrots. Melt the butter in a flame-proof casserole and fry the onions till browned. Add pork and cook till brown all over. Add any remaining flour and cook for 1 minute.

Gradually add the red wine and stock and bring to the boil, stirring constantly. Add the carrots, prunes and bouquet garni. Season, cover and simmer for 1 hour.

Add the sultanas and simmer for a further 30 minutes till juices run clear when the meat is pierced with a skewer.

Lift the pork on to a warmed serving dish. Discard the bouquet garni and pour the sauce over. Serve immediately with creamed potatoes and buttered spinach or cabbage.

Mixed pork and bean casserole

Overall timing 3¼ hours

Freezing Not suitable

To serve 6

8 oz	Dried borlotti beans	225 g
2	Pig's ears	2
2	Pig's trotters	2
	Salt and pepper	
1 lb	Salt belly of pork rashers	450 g
1 lb	Pork spare ribs	450 g
2	Large onions	2
2 oz	Lard	50 g
2	Garlic cloves	2
3 pints	Water	1.7 litres
2	Sprigs of rosemary	2
2 tbsp	Tomato purée	2x15 ml

Put beans into a saucepan of cold water and bring to the boil. Boil for 2 minutes, then remove from heat, and soak for 2 hours.

Meanwhile, singe ears and trotters if necessary. Scrub, rub with salt and wash thoroughly in cold water. Chop trotters into four lengthways; cut ears in half; halve pork rashers. Chop spare ribs in half across ribs, then cut between bones to separate them.

Peel and thinly slice onions. Melt lard in saucepan and fry onions till transparent. Add all pork and fry till golden. Add peeled and crushed garlic, water, rosemary and seasoning. Cover and simmer for 1 hour.

Drain beans; stir into pan with tomato purée. Continue simmering, uncovered, for 1 hour till beans are tender and liquid reduced by two-thirds.

Lift out meat and beans with a draining spoon and arrange on a warmed serving dish. Pour cooking liquor into a warmed sauceboat.

Auvergne lentil casserole

Overall timing 2 hours

Freezing Not suitable

To serve 6

12 oz	Continental lentils	350 g
3	Onions	3
2	Carrots	2
2	Parsnips	2
2	Leeks	2
	Bouquet garni	
12 oz	Lean pork	350 g
12 oz	Potatoes	350 g
$\frac{3}{4}$ pint	Stock	400 ml
	Salt and pepper	
8 oz	Small salami sausage	225 g
$\frac{1}{2}$ teasp	Paprika	2.5 ml

Wash and pick over lentils. Put into a flame-proof casserole and cover with cold water. Bring to the boil, cover and simmer for 30 minutes.

Peel and slice the onions, carrots and parsnips. Slice leeks. Add vegetables to lentils with bouquet garni and cook for a further 30 minutes, stirring occasionally to prevent sticking.

Cut pork into pieces. Peel and chop potatoes. Add pork and potatoes to pan with $\frac{1}{2}$ pint (300 ml) stock and seasoning and cook for a further 30 minutes, adding more stock if necessary. Remove bouquet garni.

Meanwhile, skin the salami. Grill it on all sides, then cut into thick slices. Serve casserole garnished with salami slices and sprinkled with paprika.

Sausage and vegetable stew

Overall timing 3¼ hours

Freezing Not suitable

To serve 6

1	White cabbage	1
3	Carrots	3
1	Leek	1
1	Bacon knuckle	1
1	Pig's knuckle	1
3½ pints	Water	2 litres
	Salt and pepper	
2	Large potatoes	2
8 oz	Sausages	225 g

Shred cabbage. Peel and chop carrots. Trim and slice leek. Put vegetables into a pan with the knuckles, water and seasoning. Bring to the boil, then cover and cook for 2½ hours.

Remove knuckles from pan and cut meat from bones. Peel potatoes and cut into large chunks. Cut sausages in half. Add meat, potatoes and sausages to pan and cook for a further 30 minutes. Taste and adjust seasoning before serving.

Pork with bananas and peanuts

Overall timing 1¾ hours

Freezing Not suitable

To serve 4

12 oz	Onions	350 g
2	Garlic cloves	2
4 tbsp	Oil	4x15 ml
2 lb	Pork (top of belly)	900 g
3 oz	Rice	75 g
14 oz	Can of tomatoes	397 g
1	Chicken stock cube	1
¼ teasp	Paprika	1.25 ml
¼ teasp	Ground cinnamon	1.25 ml
8 oz	Potatoes	225 g
2	Bananas	2
2 oz	Salted peanuts	50 g
	Salt	

Peel and chop onions. Peel and crush garlic. Heat 2 tbsp (2x15 ml) of the oil in saucepan. Add onions and garlic and fry until browned.

Cut pork into cubes and add to pan with rice. Cook till rice has absorbed oil, stirring frequently to prevent sticking. Add a little water if necessary to prevent burning. Remove from heat.

Pour juice from canned tomatoes into jug. Crumble in stock cube and make up to ¾ pint (400 ml) with boiling water. Chop tomatoes and add to pan with stock mixture, paprika and cinnamon. Cover and simmer gently for 20 minutes.

Meanwhile, peel and cube potatoes. Heat remaining oil in a frying pan and fry potatoes over a low heat for about 10 minutes. Add them to the pan. Peel and slice bananas and stir into the stew with the peanuts. Cook for 10 minutes. Taste and add salt if necessary.

Pork and chestnut casserole

Overall timing 1½ hours

Freezing Not suitable

To serve 6

2 lb	Lean pork	900 g
1 oz	Lard	25 g
1	Onion	1
1	Garlic clove	1
2 tbsp	Plain flour	2x15 ml
¼ pint	Dry white wine	150 ml
1 pint	Chicken stock	560 ml
	Salt and pepper	
12 oz	Chestnuts	350 g
2 oz	Butter	50 g
8 oz	Canned chickpeas	225 g
2 tbsp	Sultanas	2x15 ml

Preheat the oven to 375°F (190°C) Gas 5.

Cut the pork into bite-size pieces. Melt the lard in a flameproof casserole and fry the pork quickly till browned on all sides.

Peel and chop the onion. Peel and crush the garlic. Add to the pan and fry for 5 minutes. Stir in the flour and cook for 1 minute. Gradually add the wine and stock and bring to the boil, stirring constantly. Season, cover and cook in the oven for 45 minutes.

Meanwhile, slit the chestnuts from the base to the point. Cook in boiling water for 5 minutes, then drain and remove shells and skins.

Melt the butter in a frying pan and fry the chestnuts for 15 minutes over a medium heat till golden. Season and stir into the casserole with the drained chickpeas and sultanas. Cover and simmer for a further 15 minutes. Serve from the casserole with saffron rice and a tomato and olive salad.

Pork with cabbage

Overall timing 1 hour

Freezing Not suitable

To serve 4

1½ lb	Pork fillet	700 g
1 tbsp	Oil	15 ml
3 oz	Butter	75 g
1½ lb	Cabbage	700 g
2	Large onions	2
2 oz	Button mushrooms	50 g
1 tbsp	Plain flour	15 ml
¼ pint	Light stock	150 ml
1 tbsp	Vinegar	15 ml
6	Gherkins	6
8	Stoned green olives	8
	Salt and pepper	

Cut the pork across the grain into eight slices. Place between sheets of dampened greaseproof paper and bat out till half as thick. Heat the oil and half the butter in a flameproof casserole and fry the pork slices for 2–3 minutes each side. Remove from the pan and reserve.

Thinly slice the cabbage. Peel and thinly slice the onions. Melt the remaining butter in casserole and fry the onions and cabbage for 10 minutes. Add the halved mushrooms and fry for 3 minutes. Stir in the flour and cook for 1 minute. Gradually stir in the stock and vinegar and bring to the boil, stirring constantly. Slice the gherkins and add to the pan with the olives. Season to taste.

Arrange the meat on top of the cabbage mixture and bring to the boil. Cover tightly and simmer for 15 minutes. Serve with sauté potatoes and a tomato salad.

Russian pork chop casserole

Overall timing 30 minutes

Freezing Not suitable

To serve 4

1 lb	Potatoes	450 g
2 tbsp	Oil	2x15 ml
4	Pork rib chops	4
	Salt and pepper	
3 tbsp	Water	3x15 ml
4 oz	Button mushrooms	125 g
1 teasp	Garlic salt	5 ml
$\frac{1}{4}$ pint	Carton of soured cream	150 ml
2 tbsp	Chopped parsley	2x15 ml

Peel potatoes and cut them into very small, thin pieces. Melt the oil in a flameproof casserole and fry the potatoes for 5 minutes. Remove from pan with draining spoon.

Season chops with salt and pepper. Add to casserole and cook for 1 minute on each side. Drain off excess fat. Add water, cover and cook for 10 minutes.

Slice mushrooms. Add to casserole with fried potatoes and garlic salt and cook for a further 10 minutes. Stir in soured cream and 1 tbsp (15 ml) of the chopped parsley. Heat through. Sprinkle with remaining parsley just before serving.

Pork cassoulet

Overall timing $3\frac{1}{4}$ hours plus soaking

Freezing Not suitable

To serve 6

1 lb	Dried haricot beans	450 g
1	Pig's trotter	1
4 oz	Pork rind	125 g
2	Garlic cloves	2
2	Carrots	2
2	Onions	2
	Bouquet garni	
8 oz	Italian salami	225 g
	Salt and pepper	
2 tbsp	Oil	2x15 ml
14 oz	Can of tomatoes	397 g
1 oz	Fresh breadcrumbs	25 g

Soak beans overnight.

Quarter trotter lengthways. Chop pork rind. Add to beans with peeled garlic, carrots, one onion and bouquet garni. Cover with water, cover and simmer for $1\frac{1}{4}$ hours.

Peel salami, prick and add to pan with seasoning. Cook for 15 minutes.

Chop remaining onion. Heat oil in a saucepan and fry onion till transparent. Add 1 pint (560 ml) water, tomatoes and seasoning. Simmer for 10 minutes.

Preheat the oven to 350°F (180°C) Gas 4.

Drain beans, reserving pork rind. Add sausage and trotter to other pan. Line deep ovenproof dish with pork rind. Add layers of beans and meat mixture; top with crumbs. Bake for 30 minutes.

Rib and bean stew

Overall timing $1\frac{1}{2}$ hours plus soaking

Freezing Not suitable

To serve 4–6

8 oz	Dried borlotti beans	225 g
2	Carrots	2
2	Stalks of celery	2
2	Bay leaves	2
2 lb	Pork spare ribs	900 g
2	Large onions	2
4 tbsp	Oil	4x15 ml
14 oz	Can of tomatoes	397 g
4 tbsp	Tomato purée	4x15 ml
1 tbsp	Sugar	15 ml
$\frac{3}{4}$ pint	Chicken stock	400 ml
	Salt and pepper	

Soak beans overnight, then drain and cover with fresh water. Slice carrots and celery and add to beans with bay leaves. Simmer for 1 hour.

Separate ribs. Peel and finely chop onions. Heat oil in saucepan and fry onions till transparent. Add ribs and brown all over. Add tomatoes, tomato purée, sugar and stock and bring to the boil.

Drain beans and add to meat. Season and simmer for 15 minutes till meat is tender and cooking liquor is thick.

Finnish meat stew

Overall timing 3½ hours

Freezing Suitable

To serve 6

1 lb	Stewing beef	450 g
1 lb	Lean pork	450 g
1 lb	Boned shoulder of lamb	450 g
1 lb	Onions	450 g
1 teasp	Ground allspice	5 ml
	Salt and pepper	
¾ pint	Beef stock	400 ml

Preheat the oven to 325°F (170°C) Gas 3.

Trim the meats but don't remove all lamb fat. Cut meats into 1 inch (2.5 cm) cubes, but keep them separate. Peel and slice onions.

Spread half the beef over bottom of casserole and sprinkle with ¼ teasp (1.25 ml) allspice and seasoning. Cover with a quarter of the onions and half the pork, ¼ teasp (1.25 ml) allspice and seasoning. Repeat layering, then top with lamb.

Pour over the stock. Cook in the oven, uncovered, for about 3 hours till the meat is tender and some of the liquid has evaporated. Serve immediately with large gherkins and creamy mashed potatoes.

Old German casserole

Overall timing 1¼ hours

Freezing Suitable: add potatoes after reheating

To serve 4

4	Chicken legs	4
	Salt and pepper	
4	Onions	4
4 oz	Streaky bacon	125 g
2 oz	Butter	50 g
1½ lb	Potatoes	700 g
4 tbsp	Oil	4x15 ml
8 oz	Button mushrooms	225 g
8 oz	Pig's liver	225 g
	Plain flour	
12 oz	Pork fillet	350 g

Season chicken legs. Peel and slice onions. Derind and chop bacon. Melt butter in saucepan and fry bacon. Add onions and cook till golden. Add chicken and brown on all sides. Cover and cook gently for 30 minutes.

Peel and chop potatoes. Cook for 5 minutes in boiling salted water. Drain. Heat oil in frying pan, add potatoes and fry till crisp and golden brown all over. Drain and sprinkle with salt.

Slice mushrooms. Fry for 2 minutes, then remove from pan. Slice liver thinly and coat with seasoned flour. Cut pork into four pieces and season. Fry both for 5 minutes on each side. Add to chicken with mushrooms and potatoes. Cook for 15 minutes.

Traditional cassoulet

Overall timing 3½ hours plus 12 hours soaking

Freezing Suitable: add breadcrumbs and bake after thawing

To serve 6–8

1 lb	Dried haricot beans	450 g
1 lb	Belly of pork	450 g
4	Medium onions	4
6	Cloves	6
2	Carrots	2
2	Garlic cloves	2
2	Bouquet garni	2
2 pints	Stock	1.1 litre
1 lb	Boned lamb	450 g
1 oz	Lard	25 g
14 oz	Can of tomatoes	397 g
2 tbsp	Tomato purée	2x15 ml
	Salt and pepper	
1 lb	Garlic sausage	450 g
4 oz	Breadcrumbs	125 g

Soak beans overnight. Drain. Derind and dice belly pork. Peel two onions and spike each with cloves. Peel and chop carrots. Crush garlic. Put all into pan with one bouquet garni and stock. Cover and simmer for 1 hour.

Cube lamb. Peel and chop remaining onions. Melt lard in a saucepan and brown lamb and onions. Stir in tomatoes, tomato purée, remaining bouquet garni and seasoning. Cover and simmer for 30 minutes.

Preheat the oven to 325°F (170°C) Gas 3.

Remove spiked onions and bouquet garni from beans. Using a draining spoon, place a layer of beans in greased ovenproof casserole. Cover with half lamb mixture. Dice sausage and put half on top. Continue layers, finishing with beans. Pour over stock from beans; reserve rest. Sprinkle crumbs on top and bake for 1 hour 40 minutes. Add a little more stock if the cassoulet becomes too dry.

Polish stew

Overall timing 3¼ hours

Freezing Not suitable

To serve 8

2	Dried mushrooms	2
8 oz	White cabbage	225 g
	Salt and pepper	
1 lb 13 oz	Can of sauerkraut	820 g
1	Large onion	1
1	Cooking apple	1
4 oz	Butter	125 g
3	Large tomatoes	3
1 lb	Chuck steak	450 g
12 oz	Lean pork	350 g
8 oz	Lean lamb	225 g
6 oz	Boned chicken	175 g
2 tbsp	Oil	2x15 ml
¼ pint	Chicken stock	150 ml
¼ teasp	Ground allspice	1.25 ml
2 tbsp	Tomato purée	2x15 ml

Soak mushrooms in ¼ pint (150 ml) boiling water for 30 minutes. Shred cabbage. Blanch in boiling salted water for 2 minutes. Drain and mix with sauerkraut.

Peel and chop onion and apple. Fry in half butter till transparent. Blanch, peel and chop tomatoes. Drain mushrooms, reserving liquid, and slice thinly. Add to pan with tomatoes; cook for 3 minutes. Stir into sauerkraut with reserved liquid and seasoning.

Preheat the oven to 350°F (180°C) Gas 4. Cube meats. Melt remaining butter in pan with oil and brown meats. Remove from pan. Add stock, allspice, tomato purée and seasoning to pan and stir well. Remove from heat.

Make layers of sauerkraut mixture and meats in casserole. Pour in stock mixture. Cover tightly and bake for 1½ hours. Uncover and bake for a further 30 minutes.

Mixed meat casserole

Overall timing 2 hours 20 minutes

Freezing Not suitable

To serve 8

½	Ovenready chicken	½
1 lb	Boned best end of neck of lamb	450 g
1 lb	Lean pork	450 g
1 lb	Chuck steak	450 g
	Salt and pepper	
8 oz	Raw prawns	225 g
8 oz	Spinach	225 g
14 oz	Can of tomatoes	397 g
1 tbsp	Oil	15 ml
¾ pint	Chicken stock or water	400 ml

Preheat the oven to 325°F (170°C) Gas 3.

Cut the chicken into serving pieces. Cut the lamb, pork and beef into 2 inch (5 cm) cubes. Arrange in a casserole and season well.

Shell the prawns. Wash spinach. Drain tomatoes. Arrange all on top of the meat. Sprinkle with the oil and seasoning. Pour the stock or water over, cover tightly and cook in the oven for 2 hours till the meats are tender.

Stir the casserole and adjust the seasoning before serving with plain boiled rice.

Bohemian goulash

Overall timing 2¼ hours

Freezing Suitable: add cream after reheating

To serve 4

8 oz	Boned shoulder of lamb	225 g
8 oz	Belly pork	225 g
8 oz	Chuck steak	225 g
2 oz	Butter	50 g
2	Onions	2
3	Garlic cloves	3
2 teasp	Paprika	2x5 ml
	Bouquet garni	
1 tbsp	Tomato purée	15 ml
	Salt and pepper	
¼ pint	Carton of soured cream	150 ml

Cut meats into chunks. Melt the butter in a flameproof casserole and brown the meats on all sides.

Peel and slice the onions. Peel and crush the garlic. Add both to the casserole and cook gently till golden brown. Stir in the paprika and cook for 2 minutes.

Add bouquet garni, tomato purée and seasoning. Cover with water and bring to the boil. Cover and simmer for 1½–2 hours.

Discard bouquet garni; adjust seasoning. Stir in soured cream and serve with boiled new potatoes and a crisp green salad.

South American casserole

Overall timing 3½ hours plus overnight soaking

Freezing Not suitable

To serve 10–12

1 lb	Dried black beans	450 g
1 lb	Pork spare ribs	450 g
1 lb	Belly of pork	450 g
1 lb	Chuck steak	450 g
2	Large onions	2
2 oz	Lard	50 g
3	Garlic cloves	3
14 oz	Can of tomatoes	397 g
2	Fresh chillies	2
	Salt and pepper	
1 lb	Garlic sausage	450 g
1 lb	Pork sausages	450 g
1	Large orange	1

Soak beans overnight. Next day, put ribs, pork and steak into large pan. Add 4 pints (2.2 litres) water and bring to the boil. Skim off any scum, cover and simmer for 1 hour.

Remove meat from pan and reserve. Add drained beans to liquor and simmer for 1 hour.

Peel and chop onions. Melt lard in saucepan and fry onions till golden. Add peeled and crushed garlic, tomatoes, one-quarter of beans and ½ pint (300 ml) of cooking liquor. Deseed and slice chillies and add to pan. Season, cover and simmer for 30 minutes.

Add cooked meats and garlic and fresh sausages to remaining beans and liquor. Cover and simmer for a further 30 minutes. Lift out meats and cut into neat serving pieces. Keep hot.

Mash beans in tomato mixture till smooth, then add to beans in other pan. Taste and adjust seasoning. Pour into a warmed serving dish and arrange meats on top. Peel and slice orange for garnish.

Argentinian bollito misto

Overall timing 2¼ hours plus overnight soaking

Freezing Not suitable

To serve 6–8

4 oz	Dried chickpeas	125 g
5 pints	Water	2.8 litres
2 lb	Stewing beef	900 g
8 oz	Belly of pork	225 g
2 lb	Chicken portions	900 g
8 oz	Carrots	225 g
8 oz	Onions	225 g
3	Garlic cloves	3
½	Savoy cabbage	½
1 lb	Leeks	450 g
1 lb	Potatoes	450 g
	Salt and pepper	
2	Small spicy salami sausages	2
8	Small tomatoes	8

Soak the chickpeas in cold water overnight. The next day, drain chickpeas and put into a large flameproof casserole. Cover with the water and bring to the boil.

Cut the beef into chunks. Slice the pork. Add both to casserole with chicken. Cover and simmer for 1½ hours.

Meanwhile, peel and chop carrots. Peel and quarter onions. Peel garlic cloves. Shred cabbage. Trim and slice leeks. Peel and chop potatoes. Add prepared vegetables to casserole with seasoning and cook for 20 minutes.

Cut the sausages into large pieces and add to the pan with the tomatoes. Cook for a further 20 minutes.

Arrange meats and vegetables on warmed serving dish. Strain stock. Serve stock as soup and meat and vegetables as the main course.

Mixed offal stew

Overall timing 2½ hours

Freezing Not suitable

To serve 6–8

4 oz	Pork rind	125 g
	Salt and pepper	
1 lb	Pig lights	450 g
1	Pig's heart	1
8 oz	Pig's liver	225 g
2 oz	Lard	50 g
1	Dried red chilli	1
2	Sprigs of fresh rosemary	2
1	Bay leaf	1
5 tbsp	Red wine	5x15 ml
2 tbsp	Tomato purée	2x15 ml
2 pints	Beef stock	1.1 litres

Cut the pork rind into neat pieces. Put into a saucepan of lightly salted water and bring to the boil. Cover and simmer for 10 minutes. Drain and reserve.

Trim the lights, heart and liver and cut into 1 inch (2.5 cm) pieces. Melt the lard in a large flameproof casserole. Add all the meats and fry, stirring, until browned on all sides. Crumble the chilli into the casserole. Add one of the rosemary sprigs, the bay leaf, wine, purée and stock. Mix well and season.

Bring to the boil, then cover and simmer for about 2 hours, stirring occasionally, till meats are tender. Garnish with a sprig of rosemary and serve immediately with toasted French bread, cut into chunks.

Genoese tripe

Overall timing 2¼ hours

Freezing Not suitable

To serve 6

2 lb	Dressed tripe	900 g
2 pints	Water	1.1 litres
2	Large onions	2
1	Large garlic clove	1
1 lb	Ripe tomatoes	450 ml
3 tbsp	Oil	3x15 ml
¼ pint	Dry white wine	150 ml
2 tbsp	Tomato purée	2x15 ml
1 teasp	Sugar	5 ml
	Bay leaf	
	Sprig of rosemary	
	Salt and pepper	

Cut the tripe into pieces. Put the water into a flameproof casserole, add the tripe and bring to the boil. Skim off any scum, cover and simmer for 1 hour.

Drain the tripe in a colander, reserving the liquor. Peel and finely chop the onions; peel and crush the garlic. Blanch, peel and chop the tomatoes. Heat the oil in the casserole, add the onions and fry till pale golden. Add the garlic and wine and boil till the liquid is reduced by half.

Cut the tripe into thin strips and return to the casserole with the tomatoes, tomato purée and sugar. Tie the herbs in a bunch and add to the tripe with the reserved cooking liquor. Season and bring to the boil.

Simmer for a further 45 minutes till the tripe is tender and the liquid has reduced by half. Discard the herbs, then serve with crusty bread and butter.

Hearts casseroled with potatoes and onions

Overall timing 1¾ hours

Freezing Not suitable

To serve 4

2	Calves' hearts or	2
4	Lambs' hearts	4
4 oz	Butter	125 g
1 pint	Beef stock	560 ml
	Bouquet garni	
6 oz	Streaky bacon	175 g
8 oz	Button onions	225 g
2 lb	Potatoes	900 g
2 tbsp	Oil	2 x 15 ml
	Salt and pepper	
2 tbsp	Redcurrant jelly	2 x 15 ml
1 tbsp	Chopped parsley	15 ml

Prepare hearts. Melt 2 oz (50 g) butter in saucepan, add hearts and brown on all sides. Pour in stock, add bouquet garni, cover and simmer for 1½ hours until tender.

Meanwhile, derind bacon and cut into strips. Peel onions. Peel and chop potatoes. Cook onions in boiling salted water for 5 minutes, then add potatoes and cook for a further 5 minutes. Drain well.

Melt remaining butter with oil in frying pan. Add bacon and fry till golden. Add potatoes, onions and seasoning and cook till golden brown, turning occasionally.

Remove hearts from pan and place on warmed serving dish. Keep hot. Reduce liquid in pan to about ¼ pint (150 ml), then stir in redcurrant jelly. Pour over vegetables in frying pan and cook for 2 minutes. Arrange vegetables around hearts. Spoon over cooking juices and serve sprinkled with parsley.

Lasagne with rich meat sauce

Overall timing 1½ hours plus overnight chilling

Freezing Suitable: reheat from frozen in 350°F (180°C) Gas 4 oven for 1 hour

To serve 6–8

1	Onion	1
4 oz	Cooked ham	125 g
3 oz	Butter	75 g
2 oz	Mushrooms	50 g
½ pint	Stock	300 ml
2 tbsp	Tomato purée	2x15 ml
1 teasp	Ground cinnamon	5 ml
1 teasp	Salt	5 ml
4 oz	Chicken livers	125 g
8 oz	Cooked brains	225 g
4 oz	Cooked sweetbreads	125 g
1 pint	White sauce	560 ml
12 oz	Lasagne	350 g
3 oz	Grated Parmesan cheese	75 g

Preheat the oven to 400°F (200°C) Gas 6.

Peel and finely chop onion. Chop ham. Melt 1 oz (25 g) butter in a saucepan and cook onion and ham till golden. Slice mushrooms, add to pan with a third of stock and cook for 10 minutes. Add tomato purée, remaining stock, cinnamon and salt. Remove from heat.

Chop chicken livers. Fry in 1 oz (25 g) butter till brown. Chop brains and sweetbreads. Add livers, brains and sweetbreads to ham mixture and stir well. Cook for 10 minutes, then stir in one-quarter of white sauce.

Cook lasagne in boiling salted water for 15–20 minutes till tender. Drain.

Layer lasagne, meat and white sauces and Parmesan in greased ovenproof dish, ending with white sauce and cheese. Dot top with remaining butter. Bake for 30 minutes.

Braised oxtail

Overall timing 4¼ hours

Freezing Not suitable

To serve 4

2 tbsp	Oil	2x15 ml
2 lb	Chopped oxtail	900 g
¼ pint	Dry white wine	150 ml
3 tbsp	Brandy (optional)	3x15 ml
	Salt and pepper	
4 oz	Streaky bacon	125 g
4 oz	Button onions	125 g
3	Carrots	3
2	Small turnips	2
1	Garlic clove	1
	Celery leaves	

Preheat the oven to 300°F (150°C) Gas 2.

Heat the oil in a flameproof casserole and fry the oxtail for 10 minutes, turning the pieces frequently till well browned. Pour the fat into a frying pan.

Add the wine and brandy (if using) to the oxtail. Season, cover and cook in the oven for 2½ hours.

Meanwhile, derind and dice the bacon. Peel the onions. Peel and slice the carrots and turnips. Heat the fat in the frying pan and fry the bacon and vegetables, stirring.

Peel and crush the garlic and add to the oxtail with bacon and vegetable mixture, seasoning and a handful of celery leaves. Mix well, cover and cook for a further hour till the meat is tender. Serve with creamed potatoes.

Giblet fricassee

Overall timing 1½ hours

Freezing Not suitable

To serve 4

1¼ lb	Poultry giblets	600 g
1	Onion	1
3 tbsp	Oil	3x15 ml
¾ pint	Chicken stock	400 ml
1 teasp	Ground cumin	5 ml
	Salt and pepper	
1 tbsp	Plain flour	15 ml
2	Egg yolks	2
2 tbsp	Lemon juice	2x15 ml

Chop giblets. Peel and chop onion. Heat the oil in a saucepan and fry onion till transparent. Add giblets and brown on all sides. Pour in the stock and add cumin and seasoning. Bring to the boil, cover and simmer for about 1 hour or until giblets are tender.

Blend the flour with the egg yolks and mix in the lemon juice. Stir into fricassee and cook for a further 5 minutes, stirring. Serve with creamed potatoes and a mixed salad.

Chicken Costa Rica

Overall timing 2¾ hours

Freezing Suitable

To serve 4–6

	Salt and pepper	
3 lb	Chicken joints	1.4 kg
2	Large onions	2
4 oz	Bulb of celeriac	125 g
1	Green pepper	1
8 oz	Long grain rice	225 g
8 oz	Can of tomatoes	227 g
3 oz	Stuffed olives	75 g
3 oz	Sultanas	75 g
3 oz	Pickled walnuts	75 g
	Paprika	
	Chilli powder	
2	Bottled chillies	2

Bring a large saucepan of lightly salted water to the boil. Add the chicken pieces, cover and simmer for 1 hour till tender. Lift out chicken from pan with a draining spoon and put into a dish. Spoon over just enough cooking liquor to cover and keep warm. Reserve remaining cooking liquor.

Peel and finely chop onions and celeriac. Deseed and chop pepper. Rinse and drain rice in a sieve. Add all to reserved cooking liquor and cook for 25 minutes over a low heat, stirring occasionally to prevent sticking. The rice should absorb nearly all the liquid.

Drain the tomatoes and mash the pulp. Slice the olives and add to the rice mixture with the tomatoes, sultanas and walnuts. Cook for a further 10 minutes.

Season with paprika, chilli powder, salt and pepper. Turn into a warmed dish. Arrange chicken on top. Drain and chop chillies and use to garnish.

Colombian chicken

Overall timing 1¾ hours plus overnight soaking.

Freezing Not suitable

To serve 6

6 oz	Dried chick peas	175 g
1	Large green pepper	1
2	Medium-size onions	2
4	Tomatoes	4
2 oz	Button mushrooms	2
3 lb	Chicken legs and wings	1.4 kg
1 tbsp	Plain flour	15 ml
4 tbsp	Oil	4 x 15 ml
¼ teasp	Cayenne pepper	1.25 ml
	Salt	
1	Bay leaf	1
½ pint	Red wine	300 ml

Soak chickpeas overnight. The next day, deseed and dice pepper. Peel and finely chop onions. Blanch, peel and chop tomatoes. Slice mushrooms.

Lightly coat chicken joints with flour. Heat oil in a flameproof casserole and fry the chicken on all sides until evenly browned. Add prepared vegetables, mix well and cook for 10 minutes.

Drain chickpeas and add to the casserole with the cayenne pepper, a pinch of salt, the bay leaf and wine. Cover and simmer for 45 minutes. Remove lid and cook for a further 15 minutes. Serve with green vegetables of your choice or salad.

Chicken with aubergine and tomatoes

Overall timing 50 minutes

Freezing Not suitable

To serve 4

1	Aubergine	1
	Salt and pepper	
1	Green pepper	1
2	Large onions	2
6 tbsp	Oil	6x15 ml
4	Chicken joints	4
¾ pint	Tomato juice	400 ml
12 oz	Ripe tomatoes	350 g

Slice the aubergine. Sprinkle with salt and leave for 15 minutes. Meanwhile, deseed and slice the pepper. Peel and slice the onions.

Heat the oil in a flameproof casserole, add the chicken and fry over a moderate heat, turning frequently, till browned all over. Remove from the pan and reserve.

Add the onions and pepper and fry for 5 minutes. Return the chicken to the casserole, add the tomato juice and seasoning and bring to the boil.

Rinse the aubergine and pat dry on kitchen paper. Add to the chicken, cover and simmer for 25 minutes.

Blanch, peel and quarter the tomatoes. Add to the chicken and cook for a further 5 minutes. Serve with plain boiled rice and a green salad.

Pot au feu

Overall timing 4 hours

Freezing Not suitable

To serve 6

1	Onion	1
2	Cloves	2
2	Stalks of celery	2
1 tbsp	Chopped parsley	15 ml
4 pints	Water	2.2 litres
	Salt and pepper	
1	Cow heel	1
$\frac{1}{2}$	Boiling chicken	$\frac{1}{2}$
2	Leeks	2
1	Carrot	1
2	Potatoes	2

Peel onion and spike with cloves. Chop celery. Put into a flameproof casserole with the parsley, water and seasoning. Bring to the boil, then add cow heel and chicken. Reduce heat and simmer for 3 hours, skimming occasionally.

Remove cow heel and chicken from pan. Cut meat off bones in small chunks. Trim and thinly slice leeks. Peel and slice carrot. Peel and chop potatoes.

Strain stock and return to pan. Add meat and vegetables. Bring back to the boil, then reduce heat and simmer for 30 minutes. Serve hot with toasted bread.

Chicken cooked in beer

Overall timing 1½ hours

Freezing Suitable

To serve 4

8	Chicken legs and wings	8
	Salt and pepper	
2 tbsp	Plain flour	2x15 ml
2	Onions	2
4	Carrots	4
4	Stalks of celery	4
3 oz	Butter	75 g
2 tbsp	Gin	2x15 ml
½ pint	Can of light ale	275 ml
1	Garlic clove	1
1	Bouquet garni	1
3 tbsp	Single cream	3x15 ml

Coat the chicken pieces with well seasoned flour. Peel and quarter onions. Peel and slice carrots. Slice celery diagonally.

Melt butter in flameproof casserole, add the vegetables and cook gently for 5 minutes. Lift vegetables out with a draining spoon and set aside.

Add the chicken to the casserole and cook until golden brown on all sides, adding a little more butter if necessary. Pour on the gin and set alight. When flames have died down, return vegetables to the casserole with the light ale, seasoning, peeled and crushed garlic and bouquet garni. Cover and simmer gently for about 55 minutes.

Lift out chicken and vegetables on to warmed serving dish. Boil juices in casserole to reduce, then remove from heat and stir in cream. Pour over chicken and serve.

Catalan chicken

Overall timing 1½ hours

Freezing Suitable

To serve 4

2	Red peppers	2
8 oz	Onions	225 g
1 lb	Tomatoes	450 g
2	Aubergines	2
	Salt	
2 tbsp	Oil	2x15 ml
2 oz	Butter	50 g
8	Chicken legs and wings	8
1	Garlic clove	1
	Paprika	
4 fl oz	Dry white wine	120 ml

Deseed peppers and cut into strips. Peel and chop onions. Blanch, peel and quarter tomatoes. Cut aubergines into thick strips. Put aubergines in a bowl, sprinkle with salt and leave for 20 minutes.

Heat oil and butter in a flameproof casserole. Add chicken and cook till golden on all sides. Remove from pan. Add peppers and onions to casserole. Cook till onions are transparent, then add tomatoes and cook for 5 minutes more. Transfer mixture to a bowl and keep warm.

Rinse aubergines under cold water, then dry on kitchen paper. Add to casserole and cook for 10 minutes. Remove from pan.

Return chicken to casserole. Cover with tomato mixture and aubergines, peeled and crushed garlic, salt and a pinch of paprika. Pour in wine, cover and cook for 45 minutes. Serve with boiled rice.

Coq au vin

Overall timing 2½ hours plus 8 hours marination

Freezing Suitable: reduce sauce after reheating

To serve 6–8

3–3½ lb	Chicken joints	1.5 kg
5 oz	Streaky bacon	150 g
2 tbsp	Plain flour	2x15 ml
2 tbsp	Brandy	2x15 ml
2 tbsp	Tomato purée	2x15 ml
	Salt and pepper	
24	Button onions	24
2 oz	Butter	50 g
8 oz	Button mushrooms	225 g
Marinade		
1	Onion	1
1	Large carrot	1
2	Garlic cloves	2
3 tbsp	Olive oil	3x15 ml
18 fl oz	Full-bodied red wine	500 ml
	Black pepper	
	Bouquet garni	

Peel and chop onion and carrot; crush garlic. Place in polythene bag with rest of marinade ingredients and chicken. Marinate overnight.

Derind bacon and cut into small strips. Cook in flameproof casserole till fat starts to run out. Remove chicken from marinade and dry well. Add to casserole and brown all over. Sprinkle with flour and cook till brown. Heat brandy, set alight and pour over chicken. When flames have died down, add marinade, ¼ pint (150 ml) water, tomato purée and seasoning. Cover and simmer for 30 minutes.

Blanch and peel button onions. Melt butter in a saucepan and cook onions till golden brown. Drain and add to casserole. Continue cooking for 45 minutes.

Fry mushrooms in butter for 5 minutes. Drain and add to casserole. Cook for a further 15 minutes.

Hawaiian chicken

Overall timing 1 hour

Freezing Not suitable

To serve 4

3 lb	Chicken joints	1.4 kg
1	Bay leaf	1
1	Onion	1
	Salt and pepper	
3	Black peppercorns	3
$\frac{1}{2}$	Small white cabbage	$\frac{1}{2}$
4 oz	Celery	125 g
4 tbsp	Oil	4x15 ml
2 tbsp	Soy sauce	2x15 ml
2 oz	Shelled brazil nuts	50 g
$\frac{1}{2}$	Fresh pineapple *or*	$\frac{1}{2}$
8 oz	Can of pineapple chunks	227 g

Put chicken portions in pan with bay leaf, peeled and halved onion, $\frac{1}{2}$ teasp (2.5 ml) salt and peppercorns and cover with water. Bring to the boil, then simmer for 30 minutes.

Remove chicken from pan with a draining spoon. Take meat off the bones. Strain cooking liquor and reserve.

Shred cabbage. Finely chop celery. Heat the oil in the saucepan, add cabbage, celery and chicken meat and cook, stirring, for 5 minutes over a medium heat.

Add soy sauce, seasoning and nuts. Pour in $\frac{1}{2}$ pint (300 ml) of reserved liquor. Mix well and cook over a high heat for 5 minutes.

Peel and chop fresh pineapple or drain canned chunks. Stir into pan and cook for a further 3 minutes.

Cheesy chicken rolls

Overall timing 45 minutes

Freezing Not suitable

To serve 6

6	Large chicken breasts	6
	Salt and pepper	
2 teasp	Made mustard	2x5 ml
6	Thin slices of Derby cheese	6
6	Thin streaky bacon rashers	6
	Plain flour	
2 oz	Butter	50 g
2 tbsp	Oil	2x15 ml
½ pint	Light ale	300 ml
12	Stoned green olives	12

Remove skin and bones from chicken breasts. Season underside of chicken breasts and spread with mustard, then place a slice of cheese on each. Roll up and wrap a rasher of bacon around. Tie rolls firmly with string and coat lightly in flour.

Heat butter and oil in flameproof casserole. Lightly brown chicken rolls all over. Add beer, taking care that it does not fill more than half the casserole. Add more seasoning if required. Cover and simmer for 10 minutes.

Meanwhile, scald olives in boiling water. Drain well and add to casserole. Cover and simmer for 10 minutes more. Carefully remove string from chicken rolls and serve with rice or potatoes.

Chicken with turnips

Overall timing 1 hour

Freezing Not suitable

To serve 6

8 oz	Button onions	225 g
6	Saffron strands	6
3 lb	Ovenready chicken	1.4 kg
1½ lb	Small turnips	700 g
8 oz	Courgettes	225 g
2 oz	Butter	50 g
2 tbsp	Oil	2x15 ml
½ pint	Chicken stock	300 ml
4	Bay leaves	4
	Salt and pepper	

Blanch and peel onions. Soak saffron in 2 tbsp (2x15 ml) warm water. Cut chicken into 12 portions. Peel and chop turnips. Slice courgettes.

Heat butter and oil in frying pan and brown chicken pieces all over. Remove from pan with a draining spoon. Add onions and turnips and fry for 3 minutes, then add courgettes and fry for a further 2 minutes till browned.

Return chicken to pan with saffron and soaking water, stock, bay leaves and seasoning. Cover and simmer for 20 minutes till chicken is tender.

Mexican-style chicken

Overall timing 1½ hours plus soaking

Freezing Not suitable

To serve 4

4 oz	Dried haricot beans	125 g
6 tbsp	Oil	6x15 ml
4	Chicken joints	4
2	Onions	2
2	Garlic cloves	2
1 teasp	Chilli powder	5 ml
8 fl oz	Hot chicken stock	225 ml
8 oz	Tomatoes	225 g
2 oz	Stuffed olives	50 g
	Salt	
	Cayenne pepper	

Soak beans in 1 pint (560 ml) water overnight in a large saucepan. The next day, simmer for 1 hour.

Heat oil in flameproof casserole and brown chicken all over. Remove from pan. Peel and chop onions; peel and crush garlic. Cook in casserole till golden. Add chilli powder and cook for 5 minutes. Return chicken with stock and simmer for 55 minutes.

Blanch, peel and chop tomatoes. Slice olives. Drain beans. Add all to casserole. Cook for 10 minutes, then season with salt and cayenne pepper.

Rabbit with prunes

Overall timing 2 hours plus marination

Freezing Not suitable

To serve 4–6

2½ lb	Ovenready rabbit	1.1 kg
1	Small onion	1
1	Bay leaf	1
½ pint	Dry white wine	300 ml
3	Carrots	3
8 oz	Belly of pork	225 g
4 oz	Plump prunes	125 g
2 tbsp	Redcurrant jelly	2x15 ml
½ pint	Hot chicken stock	300 ml
	Salt and pepper	

Cut rabbit into neat pieces. Put into a shallow dish. Peel and slice onion and add to rabbit with bay leaf and wine. Marinate overnight.

Preheat the oven to 325°F (170°C) Gas 3.

Peel and chop carrots. Derind pork and cut into strips. Lift rabbit out of marinade and place in casserole. Stone prunes and fill centres with some of pork strips. Add to casserole with carrots and rest of pork. Strain marinade over rabbit.

Stir redcurrant jelly into stock and add to casserole with seasoning. Cover tightly and bake for about 1½ hours till rabbit is tender.

Rabbit in cider

Overall timing 1½ hours

Freezing Not suitable

To serve 6

3 lb	Ovenready rabbit	1.4 kg
4 oz	Butter	125 g
5 oz	Bacon rashers	150 g
1	Large onion	1
	Salt and pepper	
2 tbsp	Plain flour	2x15 ml
1 pint	Cider	560 ml
1	Bouquet garni	1
4 fl oz	Carton of single cream	113 ml
8 oz	Mushrooms	225 g
2 tbsp	Oil	2x15 ml

Cut rabbit into largish pieces. Melt 2 oz (50 g) butter in flameproof casserole. Derind bacon and cut into thin strips. Cook in butter till golden, then remove.

Peel and finely chop onion. Add to casserole with half the remaining butter and cook till transparent. Remove.

Place pieces of rabbit in casserole and cook till golden all over. Season flour and sprinkle over rabbit. Cook gently, uncovered, for 10 minutes, turning rabbit pieces once. Meanwhile, boil the cider with the bouquet garni in saucepan for about 10 minutes.

Add onion, cider, bouquet garni and cream to rabbit. Cover and cook gently for 40 minutes.

Chop mushrooms. Melt the remaining butter with the oil in a saucepan and cook mushrooms over a high heat for 5 minutes, stirring.

Remove bouquet garni from casserole. Add bacon and mushrooms, mix well and cook for 5 more minutes. Serve with creamed potatoes.

Rabbit with tarragon cream

Overall timing 2 hours

Freezing Not suitable

To serve 6

4 tbsp	Oil	4x15 ml
2 lb	Rabbit joints	900 g
3	Large onions	3
2 oz	Butter	50 g
2 tbsp	Plain flour	2x15 ml
$\frac{1}{4}$ pint	Dry white wine	150 ml
$\frac{1}{2}$ pint	Chicken stock	300 ml
2	Sprigs of tarragon	2
$\frac{1}{4}$ pint	Carton of single cream	150 ml
	Salt and pepper	

Heat the oil in a flameproof casserole, add the rabbit and fry over a high heat till browned all over. Remove the rabbit with a draining spoon and reserve. Pour off the oil.

Peel and thickly slice the onions. Melt the butter in the casserole, add the onions and fry till golden. Sprinkle in the flour and stir over a low heat for 5–10 minutes till golden. Gradually add the wine and stock and bring to the boil, stirring constantly. Return the rabbit to the pan. Cover and simmer for about $1\frac{1}{4}$ hours till the rabbit is tender.

Strip the tarragon leaves from the sprigs. Reserve a few for garnishing; chop the rest and stir into the casserole with the cream. Season to taste and heat through gently – do not boil. Arrange on a warmed serving dish, garnish with the reserved tarragon and serve with creamed potatoes.

Rabbit and chestnut ragoût

Overall timing 1¾ hours

Freezing Not suitable

To serve 6

2½ lb	Ovenready rabbit	1.1 kg
2	Onions	2
3 tbsp	Oil	3x15 ml
1¼ pints	Hot beef stock	700 ml
8 oz	Whole chestnuts	225 g
2	Pig's kidneys	2
3 oz	Butter	75 g
2 oz	Plain flour	50 g
1 tbsp	Lemon juice	15 ml
4 tbsp	Blackcurrant juice	4x15 ml
	Salt and pepper	

Remove rabbit meat from bones and cut into bite-size pieces. Peel and chop onions. Heat oil in flameproof casserole, add rabbit and brown on all sides. Add onions and cook for 3 minutes. Add ½ pint (300 ml) stock. Cover and simmer for 30 minutes.

Score round each chestnut from base to pointed end. Cook in boiling water for 5–10 minutes. Drain, then remove shells and skins.

Bring remaining stock to the boil in pan, add chestnuts and simmer for 20 minutes till tender.

Core and thinly slice kidneys. Melt 1 oz (25 g) butter in a frying pan, add kidneys and fry till browned all over.

Drain chestnuts, reserving stock. Add to rabbit with kidneys and pan juices. Melt remaining butter, add flour and cook, stirring, till golden. Gradually add reserved stock and bring to the boil, stirring. Add to rabbit mixture with lemon and blackcurrant juices and seasoning. Cook for a further 10 minutes.

Rabbit in brandy sauce

Overall timing 1¾ hours

Freezing Not suitable

To serve 6

2½ lb	Ovenready rabbit	1.1 kg
	Salt and pepper	
5 tbsp	Plain flour	5x15 ml
2	Medium-size onions	2
2	Garlic cloves	2
8 oz	Smoked streaky bacon rashers	225 g
2 oz	Butter	50 g
2 tbsp	Oil	2x15 ml
4 oz	Button mushrooms	125 g
¾ pint	Beef stock	400 ml
1 tbsp	Tomato purée	15 ml
6 tbsp	Brandy	6x15 ml
	Bay leaf	
	Sprig of thyme	

Cut rabbit into neat pieces. Season flour and use to coat rabbit. Reserve any remaining flour. Peel and thinly slice onions; peel and crush garlic. Derind bacon and cut into thin strips.

Heat butter and oil in flameproof casserole, add rabbit and brown all over. Remove from pan.

Add bacon to casserole and fry till fat runs. Add onions, garlic and mushrooms and fry, stirring occasionally, for 5 minutes. Sprinkle in remaining flour and cook for 1 minute. Gradually add stock and bring to the boil, stirring. Stir in tomato purée, brandy and seasoning. Return rabbit to casserole with bay leaf and thyme. Cover and simmer for 1 hour till rabbit is tender.

Rabbit with creamed spinach

Overall timing 2 hours

Freezing Not suitable

To serve 6

8 oz	Button onions	225 g
4 oz	Streaky bacon	125 g
3 lb	Ovenready rabbit	1.4 kg
	Salt and pepper	
3 tbsp	Plain flour	3x15 ml
3 oz	Butter	75 g
$\frac{3}{4}$ pint	Chicken stock	400 ml
4 oz	Spinach	125 g
$\frac{1}{4}$ pint	Carton of single cream	150 ml
1	Egg yolk	1

Blanch and peel onions. Derind and dice bacon. Cut rabbit into neat pieces. Season flour and use to coat rabbit. Reserve excess flour.

Melt 2 oz (50 g) butter in flameproof casserole, add rabbit and brown all over. Remove rabbit from pan.

Add bacon and onions to casserole and fry till golden. Stir in reserved flour and cook for 1 minute. Gradually add stock and seasoning and bring to the boil, stirring. Return rabbit to casserole. Cover and simmer for 1$\frac{1}{4}$ hours till rabbit is tender.

Shred spinach. Melt remaining butter in a saucepan, add spinach and cook for 3–4 minutes. Remove from heat.

Lift rabbit and onions out of casserole and arrange on a warmed serving dish. Keep hot. Add spinach to cooking liquor with cream and egg yolk and heat through gently, stirring. Pour over rabbit.

Spanish rabbit in milk

Overall timing 2 hours

Freezing Not suitable

To serve 6

3 lb	Rabbit joints	1.4 kg
2 tbsp	Plain flour	2x15 ml
4 oz	Belly of pork	125 g
2 tbsp	Oil	2x15 ml
1	Onion	1
2	Garlic cloves	2
2	Tomatoes	2
4 oz	Ground almonds	125 g
2 tbsp	Brandy	2x15 ml
	Salt and pepper	
$\frac{1}{4}$ teasp	Paprika	1.25 ml
$\frac{3}{4}$ pint	Milk	400 ml
	Parsley	

Cut the rabbit into neat pieces and toss in the flour. Derind and slice belly pork.

Heat the oil in flameproof casserole. Add belly pork and fry till browned. Add rabbit pieces and fry for 10 minutes. Remove from the pan and reserve.

Peel and chop the onion. Peel and crush the garlic. Blanch, peel and chop tomatoes. Add all to pan with ground almonds.

Return rabbit pieces to pan with brandy, a pinch of salt, the paprika and milk. Bring just to the boil. Cover and simmer for about 1½ hours, till the rabbit is tender and the sauce is thickened. Garnish with parsley. Serve with new potatoes and peas or Brussels sprouts.

Rabbit carbonnade

Overall timing 2½ hours

Freezing Not suitable

To serve 4–6

2½ lb	Ovenready rabbit	1.1 kg
3 tbsp	Plain flour	3 x 15 ml
2	Carrots	2
1	Onion	1
4 oz	Streaky bacon rashers	125 g
2 oz	Butter	50 g
	Bouquet garni	
1	Garlic clove	1
	Salt and pepper	
1 pint	Pale ale	560 ml

Preheat the oven to 350°F (180°C) Gas 4.

Cut the rabbit into neat pieces. Toss in the flour till lightly coated.

Peel and thinly slice the carrots. Peel and chop the onion. Derind the bacon and cut into strips. Melt the butter in a flameproof casserole and fry the carrots, onion and bacon for 5 minutes. Add the rabbit pieces and fry till browned.

Add the bouquet garni, peeled and crushed garlic and seasoning. Pour the ale over, cover tightly and cook in the oven for 1¾–2 hours till the rabbit is tender. Serve with boiled potatoes.

Hare casserole

Overall timing 3 hours plus 1 day's marination

Freezing Suitable

To serve 6

1	Ovenready hare with blood and liver	1
1	Garlic clove	1
1	Stalk of celery	1
1	Carrot	1
2	Bay leaves	2
	Sprig of rosemary	
3	Cloves	3
6	Juniper berries	6
	Ground cinnamon	
	Dried marjoram	
1¾ pints	Red wine	1 litre
1	Large onion	1
2 oz	Lard	50 g
2 oz	Butter	50 g
	Salt and pepper	

Cut hare into fairly large pieces, removing sinews, and place in bowl with blood. Peel and crush garlic. Slice celery. Peel and slice carrot. Add to hare with bay leaves, rosemary, cloves, juniper berries, pinches of cinnamon and marjoram and red wine. Marinate for 24 hours.

Drain hare and pat dry. Strain marinade. Peel and slice onion. Melt lard and butter in flameproof casserole and fry onion till golden. Add hare and brown all over. Add marinade, cover and simmer for 30 minutes.

Chop liver. Add to casserole with seasoning and cook for 1¾ hours more. Remove hare and vegetables from pan with draining spoon and arrange on a warmed, serving dish. Boil cooking juices rapidly till reduced by half, then strain into sauce boat.

Goose with fennel

Overall timing 2 hours

Freezing Not suitable

To serve 6

8 oz	Carrots	225 g
3	Bulbs of fennel	3
1	Garlic clove	1
1 oz	Butter	25 g
8 lb	Goose (cut into joints)	3.6 kg
3 tbsp	Plain flour	3x15 ml
1½ pints	Stock	850 ml
1 teasp	Dried thyme	5 ml
4	Bay leaves	4
	Salt and pepper	
1 lb	Potatoes	450 g
8 oz	Button onions	225 g
1 tbsp	Chopped parsley	15 ml

Peel and chop carrots. Trim fennel, then cut each bulb into four. Peel and crush garlic.

Melt the butter in a flameproof casserole, add goose portions and fry until golden. Add carrots, fennel and garlic and cook for 5 minutes.

Sprinkle flour into casserole and cook, stirring, for 2 minutes. Gradually add stock and bring to the boil, stirring. Add thyme, bay leaves and seasoning. Cook gently for about 1 hour.

Peel potatoes and cut into large chunks. Peel onions. Add both to the casserole and cook for a further 30 minutes. Adjust seasoning and stir in chopped parsley before serving.

Valencian duck

Overall timing 2½ hours

Freezing Not suitable

To serve 4–6

2	Onions	2
2	Garlic cloves	2
6 tbsp	Oil	6x15 ml
12 oz	Lean pork	350 g
4 oz	Garlic sausage	125 g
3 lb	Duck joints	1.4 kg
4	Tomatoes	4
1	Green pepper	1
	Salt and pepper	
2 teasp	Paprika	2x5 ml
8 oz	Cauliflower florets	225 g
1¾ pints	Chicken stock	1 litre
8 oz	Long grain rice	225 g
½ teasp	Saffron powder	2.5 ml
12	Cooked prawns	12
8 oz	Frozen green beans	225 g
8 oz	Frozen petits pois	225 g

Peel and slice onions; peel and crush garlic. Heat half oil in flameproof casserole and cook onions and garlic till transparent. Remove from pan.

Cut pork into large cubes; slice sausage. Add with duck to casserole and fry, turning frequently, till golden all over. Return onions and garlic to casserole.

Blanch, peel and chop tomatoes; deseed and slice pepper. Add to casserole with seasoning, paprika, cauliflower and stock and simmer for 20 minutes.

Heat remaining oil in a frying pan. Add rice and saffron and stir into oil for a few minutes. Add to casserole with unshelled prawns, beans and peas. Cover and cook for 25 minutes until rice is tender and stock has been absorbed.

Duck in creamy mushroom sauce

Overall timing 2¼ hours

Freezing Suitable: add cream after reheating

To serve 4

3½ lb	Ovenready duck	1.6 kg
	Salt and pepper	
4 oz	Celery	125 g
1	Onion	1
2 oz	Butter	50 g
½ pint	Chicken stock	300 ml
½ pint	Dry white wine	300 ml
4 oz	Button mushrooms	125 g
2 oz	Plain flour	50 g
2 tbsp	Single cream	2 x 15 ml
2 tbsp	Brandy (optional)	2 x 15 ml
	Parsley	

Preheat the oven to 400°F (200°C) Gas 6.

Season duck inside and out. Prick all over with a fork. Place duck on wire rack in roasting tin and roast for 1 hour.

Cool duck, then remove all meat from carcass. Chop into bite-size pieces. Chop celery. Peel and chop onion. Melt 1 oz (25 g) butter in a saucepan and fry celery and onion till transparent.

Break up duck carcass and add to pan with stock and wine. Cover and simmer for 30 minutes. Strain and reserve stock.

Melt remaining butter in a saucepan, add mushrooms and cook for 5 minutes. Stir in flour and cook gently for 2 minutes. Gradually stir in stock, bring to the boil, stirring, and simmer for 3 minutes. Add cream, brandy, if used, seasoning and chopped meat. Cook 10 minutes more without boiling. Serve garnished with parsley.

German-style braised partridges

Overall timing 1 hour

Freezing Not suitable

To serve 6

6	Ovenready partridges	6
	Salt and pepper	
6	Streaky bacon rashers	6
12 oz	Carrots	350 g
2	Onions	2
3 oz	Butter	75 g
1 tbsp	Chopped parsley	15 ml
1 teasp	Chopped fresh basil	5 ml
1 teasp	Chopped fresh sage	5 ml
1	Bay leaf	1
$\frac{1}{2}$ pint	Light stock	300 ml
4 tbsp	Brandy	4x15 ml
2 teasp	Cornflour	2x5 ml
$\frac{1}{4}$ pint	Carton of soured cream	150 ml

Season partridges inside and out. Wrap a bacon rasher around each and secure with a wooden cocktail stick. Peel carrots and cut into matchsticks. Peel and chop onions. Melt butter in flameproof casserole and brown partridges quickly on all sides. Remove from pan.

Add carrots and onions to casserole and fry for 3 minutes. Return partridges to pan with herbs, stock and seasoning. Cover and simmer for 30 minutes till partridges are tender.

Remove from heat. Warm brandy in ladle, ignite and pour over partridges. When flames have died down, strain cooking liquor into a saucepan. Blend cornflour with 2 tbsp (2x15 ml) cold water and stir into liquor. Bring to the boil, stirring. Add soured cream and heat through gently. Serve sauce with partridges.

Guinea fowl in red wine

Overall timing 1½ hours

Freezing Not suitable

To serve 4

2	Ovenready guinea fowl	2
	Salt and pepper	
2	Onions	2
2 oz	Butter	50 g
1 tbsp	Plain flour	15 ml
1 pint	Red wine	560 ml
4 oz	Cooked ham	125 g
	Grated nutmeg	
4 oz	Pork sausagemeat	125 g
4 oz	Mushrooms	125 g

Cut the guinea fowl into portions. Season with salt and pepper. Peel and chop the onions. Melt half the butter in a flameproof casserole and fry the onions till transparent. Add guinea fowl portions and fry quickly till browned all over.

Sprinkle in the flour and fry for 2 minutes. Gradually stir in the wine and bring to the boil, stirring. Chop the ham and add to the casserole with nutmeg and pepper. Reduce heat, cover and cook gently for 45 minutes till guinea fowl are tender.

Meanwhile melt remaining butter in frying pan, add sausagemeat and fry gently until just golden, stirring frequently to break it up into small pieces. Slice the mushrooms, add to the pan and cook for a few minutes more.

Remove guinea fowl from casserole. Arrange on a warmed serving dish and keep hot. Add sausagemeat mixture to sauce and simmer for 5 minutes, mixing well. Adjust seasoning, then spoon sauce over guinea fowl and serve.

Pigeons with saffron

Overall timing 1 hour

Freezing Not suitable

To serve 6

3	Ovenready pigeons	3
	Salt and pepper	
1 tbsp	Plain flour	15 ml
1 tbsp	Oil	15 ml
2 oz	Butter	50 g
6	Saffron strands	6
3 tbsp	Lemon juice	3x15 ml
1	Small onion	1
2 tbsp	Chopped parsley	2x15 ml

Quarter the pigeons. Lightly coat with seasoned flour. Heat the oil and butter in a saucepan, add the pigeon pieces and fry for about 10 minutes till lightly browned on all sides.

Meanwhile, pound the saffron in a small bowl. Add 2 tbsp (2x15 ml) warm water and leave to soak for 10 minutes.

Add saffron, soaking liquid and lemon juice to the pan. Cover and cook over a low heat for 20 minutes till meat is tender. Remove pigeon pieces from the pan, place on a warmed serving dish and keep hot.

Peel and finely chop the onion. Add to the liquid in the pan with parsley and seasoning. Cook for 3 minutes, then spoon over the pigeon quarters and serve immediately with boiled rice.

Ratatouille

Overall timing 1½ hours

Freezing Suitable

To serve 8

2	Large aubergines	2
1 lb	Courgettes	450 g
	Salt and pepper	
3	Large onions	3
2–3	Garlic cloves	2–3
2	Green peppers	2
1 lb	Ripe tomatoes	450 g
5 tbsp	Olive oil	5x15 ml
1 teasp	Sugar	5 ml

Cut the aubergines into 1 inch (2.5 cm) chunks. Cut courgettes into quarters lengthways, then into 1 inch (2.5 cm) lengths. Put the vegetables into a colander, sprinkle with salt and leave to drain for 30 minutes.

Meanwhile, peel and slice the onions. Peel and crush the garlic. Deseed and thinly slice the peppers. Blanch, peel and halve the tomatoes.

Heat the oil in a flameproof casserole, add the onions and garlic and fry gently till transparent. Dry the aubergines and courgettes on kitchen paper and add to the pan with the peppers, tomatoes, sugar and plenty of pepper. Cook for about 45 minutes till the vegetables are tender but not mushy. Adjust the seasoning and serve hot, or cool and chill before serving.

Potato and onion bake

Overall timing 1 hour

Freezing Not suitable

To serve 4

1½ lb	Potatoes	700 g
12 oz	Onions	350 g
3 oz	Butter	75 g
	Salt and pepper	

Preheat the oven to 400°F (200°C) Gas 6.

Peel the potatoes and slice very thinly (use a mandolin for best results). Put into a bowl of cold water to prevent discoloration. Peel and thinly slice the onions.

Drain the potatoes and dry with kitchen paper. Butter an ovenproof dish and cover the bottom with a layer of potato. Dot with butter, season and cover with a layer of onion. Dot with butter, season and repeat the layers till all the ingredients have been used, finishing with potato. Dot the top with the remaining butter.

Bake for about 40 minutes till the potatoes are tender and golden. Serve immediately.

Mushroom casserole

Overall timing 2½ hours

Freezing Not suitable

To serve 4

2 lb	Flat mushrooms	900 g
1 oz	Butter	25 g
1	Onion	1
1	Garlic clove	1
8 oz	Cooked ham	225 g
8 oz	Lean pork	225 g
4 oz	Streaky bacon	125 g
4	Sprigs of parsley	4
2	Eggs	2
1 tbsp	Fresh breadcrumbs	15 ml
	Salt and pepper	
½ oz	Dripping	15 g
1 tbsp	Oil	15 ml
1 teasp	Wine or cider vinegar	5 ml

Preheat the oven to 325°F (170°C) Gas 3.

Separate mushroom stalks from the caps. Halve or quarter caps if large and reserve. Chop the stalks. Melt the butter in a saucepan, add the chopped mushroom stalks and fry over a high heat until all the liquid has evaporated. Remove pan from heat.

Peel and finely chop the onion and garlic. Mince the ham, pork, derinded bacon and parsley. Add all these ingredients to the saucepan with the eggs, breadcrumbs and generous seasoning. Mix well.

Heat the dripping and oil in flameproof casserole. When hot, remove from heat and put in a layer of the mince mixture (don't pack tightly), followed by a layer of mushroom caps. Repeat until all the ingredients have been used up. Cover and bake for about 2 hours. Sprinkle with vinegar just before serving with a mixed salad.

Sweet-sour vegetables

Overall timing 1 hour

Freezing Not suitable

To serve 6

6	Saffron strands	6
3	Bulbs of fennel	3
	Salt and pepper	
2	Large onions	2
3 tbsp	Olive oil	3x15 ml
3	Large ripe tomatoes	3
1	Orange	1
¼ pint	Dry white wine	150 ml
1 teasp	Caster sugar	5 ml

Put the saffron into a bowl with 2 tbsp (2x15 ml) warm water and leave to soak for 10 minutes.

Trim the fennel and cut each bulb into quarters. Blanch in boiling salted water for 5 minutes, then drain. Peel and slice the onions. Heat the oil in a flameproof casserole, add the onions and fry till transparent.

Blanch, peel and chop the tomatoes. Remove the rind from the orange with a potato peeler and shred finely. Squeeze the juice from the orange. Add the orange rind and juice to the pan with the tomatoes, fennel, saffron and soaking water, wine and sugar. Bring to the boil and season.

Cover tightly and simmer for about 30 minutes till vegetables are tender.

Country-style peas

Overall timing 45 minutes

Freezing Not suitable

To serve 6

4 oz	Button onions	125 g
2 lb	Fresh peas	900 g
3	Carrots	3
8 oz	New potatoes	225 g
1	Round lettuce	1
1	Thick streaky bacon rasher	1
2 oz	Butter	50 g
	Sprig of thyme	
	Sprig of tarragon	
	Bay leaf	
	Salt and pepper	

Blanch and peel onions. Shell peas; scrape and dice carrots. Scrub potatoes. Tear lettuce into pieces. Derind bacon and cut into strips.

Melt butter in a flameproof casserole and fry bacon and onions till bacon fat begins to run. Add remaining vegetables, herbs tied together, seasoning and $\frac{1}{4}$ pint (150 ml) water. Cover and simmer for 25 minutes till vegetables are tender. Remove herbs before serving.

Cheese and potato bake

Overall timing $1\frac{1}{4}$ hours

Freezing Not suitable

To serve 6

2 lb	New potatoes	900 g
3	Onions	3
2 tbsp	Oil	2 x 15 ml
1	Red pepper	1
8 oz	Sliced cooked ham	225 g
14 oz	Can of tomatoes	397 g
5	Small gherkins	5
12 oz	Red Leicester cheese	350 g
$\frac{1}{4}$ pint	Soured cream	150 ml
2	Egg yolks	2
	Salt and pepper	
$\frac{1}{4}$ teasp	Grated nutmeg	1.25 ml
2 oz	Butter	50 g

Preheat the oven to 400°F (200°C) Gas 6.

Scrub potatoes. Cook in boiling water for 30 minutes.

Peel and thinly slice onions. Fry in oil for 5 minutes. Deseed and slice red pepper, add to onion and fry for 5 minutes. Shred ham; add to pan with tomatoes, sliced gherkins and seasoning.

Drain potatoes and cool. Slice thickly. Slice cheese. Layer potatoes, cheese and tomato mixture in greased ovenproof dish. Mix soured cream, egg yolks, seasoning and nutmeg and pour over top. Dot with butter. Bake for 20 minutes.

Caponata

Overall timing 45 minutes

Freezing Suitable

To serve 4–6

8 oz	Green peppers	225 g
1½ lb	Aubergines	700 g
4 tbsp	Olive oil	4x15 ml
1	Large onion	1
3	Stalks of celery	3
8 oz	Tomatoes	225 g
4 oz	Stoned green olives	125 g
2 tbsp	Capers	2x15 ml
	Salt and pepper	
1 teasp	Caster sugar	5 ml
6 tbsp	Vinegar	6x15 ml
6 tbsp	Water	6x15 ml

Deseed and slice peppers. Chop aubergines. Heat 2 tbsp (2x15 ml) oil in a frying pan. Add peppers and aubergines and fry for 15 minutes.

Peel and chop onion; chop celery. Blanch, peel and quarter tomatoes. Heat rest of oil in another frying pan. Add onion and cook till brown. Add celery, tomatoes, olives and capers. Cook 5 minutes.

Mix in peppers and aubergines with seasoning, sugar, vinegar and water. Cover and cook gently for 15 minutes. Serve cold.

Peperonata

Overall timing 1½ hours

Freezing Suitable

To serve 4

2	Large red peppers	2
2	Large green peppers	2
1	Onion	1
4 tbsp	Olive oil	4x15 ml
6	Tomatoes	6
1	Garlic clove	1
	Salt and pepper	
12	Basil leaves	12

Deseed peppers and cut into thin strips. Peel and slice the onion. Heat oil in flameproof casserole and fry onion till golden brown. Add peppers and cook for 15 minutes.

Blanch, peel and roughly chop tomatoes. Add to the casserole with peeled garlic and seasoning. Cover and simmer over low heat for about 1 hour until all vegetables are soft.

Remove garlic, garnish with basil leaves and serve hot or cold.

Aubergine and pasta casserole

Overall timing 1 hour

Freezing Not suitable

To serve 4–6

1	Large aubergine	1
	Salt and pepper	
1	Onion	1
1	Garlic clove	1
3 oz	Butter	75 g
1 lb	Tomatoes	450 g
2 teasp	Chopped fresh basil	2x5 ml
3 fl oz	Oil	90 ml
12 oz	Rigatoni	350 g
3 oz	Mozzarella cheese	75 g

Preheat oven to 400°F (200°C) Gas 6.

Cut aubergine into thin slices lengthways. Arrange slices on a plate, sprinkle with salt and leave for 30 minutes.

Meanwhile, peel and chop onion. Peel and crush garlic. Melt 2 oz (50 g) of the butter in a saucepan, add onion and garlic and fry till transparent.

Blanch, peel and finely chop tomatoes. Add to onion with seasoning. Simmer gently for 15 minutes. Remove from heat and stir in basil.

Rinse aubergine slices under running cold water and pat dry with kitchen paper. Heat oil in frying pan, add slices and cook for 4–5 minutes each side. Drain on kitchen paper.

Cook rigatoni in boiling salted water till tender. Drain and mix with tomato sauce. Season to taste. Put half the rigatoni mixture into greased ovenproof dish and arrange aubergine slices on top. Add remaining rigatoni mixture. Thinly slice cheese and arrange on top. Dot with remaining butter and bake for 15 minutes. Serve hot.

Rumanian vegetable casserole

Overall timing 1¼ hours

Freezing Not suitable

To serve 6–8

2	Waxy potatoes	2
2	Turnips	2
2	Medium-size onions	2
2	Garlic cloves	2
2	Carrots	2
1	Medium-size aubergine	1
2	Courgettes	2
2	Small leeks	2
4 oz	French beans	125 g
3	Large tomatoes	3
1 oz	Butter	25 g
2 tbsp	Oil	2x15 ml
4 oz	Shelled fresh peas	125 g
2 tbsp	Tomato purée	2x15 ml
	Bouquet garni	
	Salt and pepper	

Peel the potatoes, turnips, onions, garlic and carrots. Cut the potatoes, turnips, carrots, aubergine and courgettes into ¾ inch (2 cm) chunks. Cut the leeks and beans into 1 inch (2.5 cm) lengths. Quarter the tomatoes; slice the onions.

Heat the butter and oil in a flameproof casserole and fry the onions, leeks and garlic till golden. Add the remaining vegetables, tomato purée, bouquet garni and 1 pint (560 ml) water and mix well. Season and bring to the boil. Simmer gently for about 45 minutes till the vegetables are tender.

Index